It's all Greek to M. E.

"I don't think you know what you're getting into," my father said. "There isn't any housing left at the university for out-of-state students. That means if you don't get asked to join a sorority, you have to come home."

He said that to me over and over that summer, but I don't think I understood what he was saying. I think if I'd really understood, I would have been too terrified to go through Rush Week at the University of Missouri.

I suppose a little of what could happen to me began to sink in when my father refused to ship my trunk on to Missouri until after Rush Week.

"If you don't make a sorority," he said, "you'll only have to ship it right back, so we'll wait and see."

Rush Week began a week before school began; so a week before the school year would be underway, I took a train to St. Louis, and then a bus to Columbia, Missouri.

On the bus I began to wonder what I'd done to myself.

Books by M. E. Kerr

Dinky Hocker Shoots Smack!
Best of the Best Books (YA) 1970–83 (ALA)
Best Children's Books of 1972, *School Library Journal*
ALA Notable Children's Books of 1972

If I Love You, Am I Trapped Forever?
Honor Book, *Book World* Children's Spring Book Festival, 1973
Outstanding Children's Books of 1973, *The New York Times*

The Son of Someone Famous
(An Ursula Nordstrom Book)
Best Children's Books of 1974, *School Library Journal*
"Best of the Best" Children's Books 1966–1978, *School Library Journal*

Is That You, Miss Blue?
(An Ursula Nordstrom Book)
Outstanding Children's Books of 1975, *The New York Times*
ALA Notable Children's Books of 1975
Best Books for Young Adults, 1975 (ALA)

Love Is a Missing Person
(An Ursula Nordstrom Book)

I'll Love You When You're More Like Me
(An Ursula Nordstrom Book)

Gentlehands
(An Ursula Nordstrom Book)
Best Books for Young Adults, 1978 (ALA)
ALA Notable Children's Books of 1978
Best Children's Books of 1978, *School Library Journal*
Winner, 1978 Christopher Award
Best Children's Books of 1978, *The New York Times*

Little Little
ALA Notable Children's Books of 1981
Best Books for Young Adults, 1981 (ALA)
Best Children's Books of 1981, *School Library Journal*
Winner, 1981 Golden Kite Award, Society of Children's Book Writers

What I Really Think of You
(A Charlotte Zolotow Book)
Best Children's Books of 1982, *School Library Journal*

Me Me Me Me Me: Not a Novel
(A Charlotte Zolotow Book)
Best Books for Young Adults, 1983 (ALA)

Him *She Loves?*
(A Charlotte Zolotow Book)

I Stay Near You
(A Charlotte Zolotow Book)
Best Books for Young Adults, 1985 (ALA)

Night Kites
(A Charlotte Zolotow Book)
Best Books for Young Adults, 1986 (ALA)
Recommended Books for Reluctant YA Readers, 1987 (ALA)

Fell
(A Charlotte Zolotow Book)
Best Books for Young Adults, 1987 (ALA)

Fell Back
(A Charlotte Zolotow Book)
Finalist, Edgar Allan Poe Award, Best Young Adult Mystery
(Mystery Writers of America)

Fell Down
(A Charlotte Zolotow Book)

Linger

ME ME ME ME ME

not a novel by M.E. Kerr

A Charlotte Zolotow Book

HarperTrophy
A Division of HarperCollins*Publishers*

for Vivienne Nearing—
dear friend and counselor

Me Me Me Me Me
Copyright © 1983 by M. E. Kerr
All rights reserved. No part of this book may be used or reproduced in any manner whatsoever without written permission except in the case of brief quotations embodied in critical articles and reviews. Manufactured in the United Kingdom by HarperCollins Publishers Ltd. For information address HarperCollins Children's Books, a division of HarperCollins Publishers, 10 East 53rd Street, New York, NY 10022.

Library of Congress Cataloging-in-Publication Data
Kerr, M. E.
  Me me me me me : not a novel.
  "A Charlotte Zolotow book"
  Summary: The author recounts escapades from her own teenage years and reveals how many of those real-life people and events served as springboards for the fictional characters and plots in her nine young adult novels.
  1. Kerr, M. E.—Biography—Youth. 2. Novelists, American—20th century—Biography. [1. Kerr, M. E. 2. Authors, American] I. Title.
PS3561.E643Z468   1983   813'.54[92]   82-48521
ISBN 0-06-023192-0
ISBN 0-06-023193-9 (lib. bdg.)
ISBN 0-06-446163-7 (pbk.)

First Harper Trophy edition, 1994.

Contents

	Author's Note	ix
1	"Murder" He Says	1
2	Where Are You Now, William Shakespeare?	35
3	Marijane the Spy	44
4	1, 2, 3, 4, 5, 6, 7, 8, 9, 10, 11, 12, 100!	59
5	There's Not a Man in This Damn Nunnery!	78
6	Your Daddy Was a Sailor	113
7	What I Did Between Trains	136
8	The Sister of Someone Famous	147
9	Rush Week	160
10	Sorority Life	176
11	New York	206

Author's Note

This is an answer to many letters from kids wanting to know if the things I write about really happened to me.

This is what really happened to me when I was a kid, as I remember it, but I've changed some names and details of other people involved in the incidents I describe.

For some reason my dad, who was a mayonnaise manufacturer in a small upstate New York town, kept a journal all his life. I couldn't have remembered everything so well without it.

"Men keep journals," my chauvinistic father told me, "and women keep diaries."

I didn't keep as good a diary as he did a journal, but I did write in my diary from time to time in my teens, and I saved old letters and stories I wrote . . . and they helped me a lot as I worked on this.

Before I sat down to write, I thought of the title *Yesterday Me*.

But as I wrote a little bit every day, I couldn't stop hearing a snide little voice in my head, calling out what I'd seen written across a T-shirt a few years back:

MEMEMEMEME

I'm calling this that.

It's dedicated to YOU YOU YOU YOU YOU kids who wrote me, and to your teachers and librarians who encouraged you to read me.

One:
"Murder" He Says

A hot Friday night in August, and I am up in my room, waiting for my date to arrive. I am listening to "Temptation" on a record that would break into small pieces if I were to drop it.

My date is due at seven.

I'm fifteen. I'm going steady.

I'm wearing a black peasant skirt, a white peasant blouse, and huaraches. My stockings are painted on, from a bottle of suntan lotion, and a fake white gardenia is pinned in my long blond hair, worn pageboy style.

I'm always dressed a half hour early, but the rule in our house is that you stay upstairs until your date arrives, and wait at least five minutes after he's inside, before you show yourself. This is to give my father time to scare him to death. This is also a way of not appearing eager.

"Always play hard to get," my father advises, "and if a boy starts to tell you a joke you've heard before, pretend you haven't heard it. Laugh hard after he tells it . . . unless it's dirty."

While I wait, I read from *The Fountainhead* by Ayn Rand. I'm not reading the whole book, just "the good parts."

He had thrown her down on the bed and she felt the blood beating in her throat, in her eyes, the hatred, the helpless terror in her body. She felt the hatred and his hands; his hands moving over her body, the hands that broke granite.

My best friend, Ella Gwen Logan, lent me the book, with "the good parts" marked.

I had to smuggle it into the house and up to my bedroom.

I've already been warned by my mother that Ella Gwen is not a good influence.

I hear the doorbell ring.

I hear my mother call out, "Come in, Donald!"

I put *The Fountainhead* back under my mattress and stand in front of my bureau mirror, combing my hair and putting on Tabu.

Donald is now entering our living room, where my father is looking over his newspaper at him, grunting a hello.

My father is president of a mayonnaise factory, now dehydrating onions for the government. The whole town stinks of onions, and this is a great embarrassment to me.

My father served in the French army, way back in World War I, and he affects a French beret, which is more embarrassment. No one else's father wears a beret.

No one else's father rides a bicycle back and forth to work in his beret.

My father does many things I think are humiliating.

He is slightly deaf and wears a tiny black plug in his left ear. When we are in church Sunday mornings, he makes a great production out of removing the plug just as the minister is about to deliver his sermon. My father pulls the plug out, reaches inside his suit jacket for the black box that goes with it, and wraps the cord around the box. At the end of the sermon, when the choir starts to sing, he takes the box out once more, unwinds the cord, and sticks the plug back into his ear.

This is the same man who sent me off to Sunday school, when I was little, with a question for my Sunday school teacher: What was the slipperiest day in Bethlehem? ("The day Joseph came through on his ass.")

Donald is now saying, "How are you tonight, sir?"

My father won't bother to answer that one.

He won't bother to put down his newspaper, either.

My father is showing Donald just what he thinks of Donald's notion that he is good enough to date my father's daughter.

My mother invites Donald to sit down, and Donald sits on the very edge of the davenport.

My mother talks to him softly.

My parents are like the classic team of police detectives handling a guileful suspect. One is rough and one is gentle.

Donald is caught between them, alternately nodding in agreement with everything my mother says and stealing nervous glances across the room at my scowling father.

Donald Dare is a local undertaker's son. He's sixteen. We've been going steady for a year, and we sign all our notes "Puddles of Purple Passion."

We have a song, too. " 'Murder' He Says." ("He says 'Murder' he says, every time we kiss. . . .")

I wear a silver identification bracelet he gave me, with "Murder" on one side and "He Says" on the other.

The only time we kiss is when we say good night at my front door. It is a very fast kiss, mouths closed along with eyes, and he has never said "Murder" after. He has never tried to French kiss—some girls call it a soul kiss. When we talk about boys, we talk about this kind of kissing. We talk about boys trying to pet "below the neck," "below the waist." Our conversations take place in the girls' toilet at school, and in our bedrooms at pajama parties.

I always greatly exaggerate the difficulty I have controlling Donald.

But Donald and I go everywhere together, keeping our hands to ourselves when we're alone, holding hands in public. We need other eyes on us to be demonstrative. We seek out the crowd and wrap our arms around each other.

I can't remember how our "romance" started.

Our friendship started with my curiosity about Dare's Funeral Home.

That was when I was fourteen. I'd go down to the funeral

parlor with Donald after school, on warm spring days when he knew he didn't have to ask me inside.

He'd never let any kids from school inside his house.

There were ramps all through the downstairs, to make it easier to roll caskets from room to room. There were always overnight "guests," all dead. There was the sickly sweet smell of too many roses, gladioli, daffodils, and lilies. There was the likelihood of running into strangers who were crying.

We would sit outside in the yard, on the iron glider, and he would complain to me.

"I'm not going to be an undertaker!"

"What's that building in the back?" I'd ask. I wanted to be a writer, and I was curious about anything that was different.

Donald's house was definitely different.

"That's the shop," he'd answer me, and he'd get red.

"Is that where they work on the bodies?"

"I won't even go back there," he'd say.

"Is that where they work on the bodies?"

"That's where they take them."

"Did you ever go back there?"

"I've been back there, but I hate it back there, and he knows it."

His father, in conversation, was always "he" or "him." Donald never said "my father."

We had a state prison in the center of our town, and Donald once said, "I'd rather be a convict's son than an undertaker's son."

"Your father should have decided to have more children,"

I said. "If you had brothers, one of them might have wanted to carry on the family business."

"No brother of mine would want to be an undertaker, either."

"But at least you'd have a better chance if you had a brother. You could flip a coin to see who'd be the undertaker."

"Well, I don't have a brother."

"If you had a sister, she'd probably have to do the cosmetic work on all the corpses, just like your mother does."

"You know what he says? He says my wife will do that. He says that's the way a family business works."

"Don't ask me to be your wife," I told him.

"I'd never ask anybody to be my wife if I planned to stay in this town," Donald said, "but I don't plan to. I'm going to get out. I'll never be an undertaker."

"I'm going to get out too," I said. "This town's too small for me."

"I really am going to get out," Donald said.

"I really am, too."

Finally either Donald got past his embarrassment over his house around me, or I wore him down with my questions.

I got to go inside.

There were all sorts of rules in that house. All the window shades had to be at the same level so it'd look good from the outside. Radios had to be played very low. Donald's mother couldn't cook anything like corned beef and cabbage that would make the house smell. All old "floral tributes" had to be removed before they began wilting.

I saw my first dead people up close, their heads resting on oversized satin pillows, hands folded one over the other as they lay stretched out in their coffins. I saw Gorilla, the Dares' fat white angora cat, who sneaked into the "slumber rooms" every chance he got, to sleep with the "guests." I sat listening to Donald's plump, rouge-cheeked mother practice "Jesus Is Tenderly Calling" on their pump organ in the parlor, next to the casket selection room. I watched his tall, burly father trudge up from "the shop" afternoons, for a cup of Lipton tea in their kitchen. He'd say he was taking a break, and I'd imagine some corpse left with the blood draining out of it, on a slab in the back building.

Donald and I got to like each other. We shared a rebel's hatred of a small town where everyone knew everything you did; we shared a palms-hitting-forehead astonishment over things parents expected you to do.

Sometimes he'd drive the hearse up to my house, and we'd sit in it and listen to the radio.

My father'd say, "I don't want you sitting in the hearse with him! Sit out in the open."

I wasn't allowed to go anywhere in a car with a boy, much less in a hearse with one.

"Oh, Ellis," my mother'd say when she thought I was out of earshot (I seldom was), "they don't *do* anything."

"It doesn't look good," he'd insist.

How Donald and I got from the glider in his yard, and the hearse in our driveway, to dances in the school gym and "Puddles of Purple Passion," I was never sure, but there he was on that August night in our downstairs, being bullied by my father.

————————

My father finally puts down his newspaper.

"Business is good tonight, Donald! Lots of obituaries in the paper. Ha! Ha! Ha!"

My father always treated Donald the way he treated Skippy, our family dog. He always spoke gruffly. ("Did you get your geometry homework done, Skippy? You can't go out if you didn't!") He always thought what he said to either of them was hilarious, but Donald and the dog didn't think so. They just sat shivering in his presence.

Donald stands up as I enter the room. His mother has drilled manners into him. ("If you're rude, people will remember it when their loved ones pass and they'll call Dowd's instead of Dare's.")

Donald's very tall, like his father—my own father has to look up to him—and he's skinny, since he claims everything that goes on in his house makes him lose his appetite. Behind his back my father says he's probably consumptive, and calls him Famine.

Donald's wearing the pants to his glen plaid double-breasted suit, a white shirt, and a gray V-neck sweater, with newly polished loafers.

He'd like to be wearing pegged pants, as the other boys are, but the only concession to modern style that his father allows is a long gold watch chain looped down the right side of his pants.

The boys stand around on downtown street corners twirling

their long watch chains. They're our town's version of zoot-suiters.

All the burden of what the only son of a funeral director feels is in Donald's very light, sad blue eyes. He often looks close to tears. He never smiles so you can see his perfect white teeth. Just a slight tip to his lips.

"Hi," he manages, and I manage "Hi" back, even though the notes we pass in school always have umpteen x's at the end. We are bolder on paper than we are face to face. We both come from families who only kiss on holidays when relatives arrive, or at airports and train stations.

Secretly, I once read a journal my father keeps, and hides behind The Harvard Classics.

One entry read:

Our daughter is dating the local undertaker's son, Donald Dare: tall, dark, and harmless. Dares very little is my guess.

My father's eyes narrow. "Donald? I want her back at twelve o'clock sharp!"

"Yes, sir. Twelve o'clock."

"Not five minutes after twelve, and not two minutes after twelve. Twelve o'clock sharp!"

My mother starts purring. "Are you going to Murray's after the movie?"

"Yes."

Murray's is the hangout, where we go to drink Cokes, listen to the jukebox, put salt in the sugar bowls, and tell the one about the traveling salesman and the farmer's daughter.

I say nothing about our plan to connect with Ella Gwen Logan and Hyman Ginzburg.

It is 1943. There is a world war raging.

My father puts ads in the local paper, apologizing for the onion smell:

Ivanhoe Foods Has Gone to War!
Our onions are for field rations for our fighting men.
When you smell onions, pray for peace.

My mother saves fats and tin.

My older brother has just been commissioned an ensign, and assigned to a carrier-based torpedo bomber squadron.

My father is an air-raid warden and patrols our neighborhood with a flashlight, wearing a special white helmet, armband, and gas mask.

I am not allowed to speak to sailors, who pour into our small town from Sampson Naval Base.

There is gas, shoe, meat, cheese, coffee, and butter rationing.

Boys who were ahead of me in high school are listed as dead or missing in the local paper.

I will remember very little of this as I grow older. But I will never forget Ella Gwen Logan and Hyman Ginzburg.

Ella Gwen's father was a dentist, in the days when going to the dentist really hurt.

Dr. Logan never made it any easier.

He was one of the meanest little men in town, the kind who chuckled when you yelled, "Now *that* hurts!" and told you it didn't hurt much.

He had a red face and darting brown eyes, no taller than
five five, with only one thing going for you if he was your
dentist, and that was his obsession with cleanliness.

He changed his little white coats after every patient, and
kept a can of 20 Mule Team Borax to scrub his hands with
every five minutes at the sink.

His radio was tuned to the local station, but you heard
very little of tunes like "Don't Get Around Much Anymore,"
"You'd Be So Nice to Come Home to," and "As Time Goes
By."

His sister, Ella Gwen's Aunt Mildred, was his nurse, and
what you heard mostly were their running conversations that
went something like this:

"I hear old man Finkelstein is selling his scrap metal to
the Japs."

"I wouldn't put it past that kike!"

Or:

"What do you mean wops don't wash their salad bowls?"

"Wops don't. They just wipe them out with a dirty cloth
after they use them, which is why I don't order salad when
I eat dago."

You'd go into his office and you'd hear about thirty minutes
of their harangues on niggers, wops, kikes, polacks, hunkies,
and spics, all the while he hit every exposed nerve he could
reach in your mouth with his little silver pick.

Ella Gwen's mother was always "sick," usually upstairs in
bed, in their house on Apple Avenue. It wasn't until I was
grown up that I discovered she drank up there. Her sickness
was the bottle, but none of us kids knew that. She never lurched

around or acted loud or slurred her words. When she did get herself downstairs in a robe, and Dr. Logan was around delivering one of his tirades, all she ever said was "Oh, Charlie." She wouldn't say it in a condemning way. There'd be this little smile on her mouth, as though he was some kind of cutup, doing and saying things anyone would who had the nerve.

From these two Ella Gwen came, which ought to knock the socks off the old saying "An apple never falls far from the tree."

Ella Gwen was as unlike her family as a peacock is unlike sheep. When we'd leave her house and all of his frothing bigotry, she'd walk beside me, flame faced, looking down, saying only, "I can't help it," in a whisper.

She was a tiny, pretty, blue-eyed blonde. The boys were always whistling at her and following her from school. But she wasn't allowed to date until she was eighteen.

She had two years to go. Her nineteen-year-old brother was a lieutenant in the Army, somewhere in England.

Ella Gwen's sex lecture from her mother had consisted of one sentence: "Your brother can come home after doing it, take a shower, and be a new man, but you would be ruined for life."

Ella Gwen put herself between all the school bullies and the ones being bullied.

When we were in sixth grade, she stuck up for a minister's son named Nelson Tutton. He was the only boy in our grade who didn't have long pants. He was fat and frightened, and he wet his pants when he was cornered by classmates. Reverend Tutton declared he'd stay in knickers until he stopped wetting. As long as he stayed in knickers, he got picked on, he got scared, he peed.

His mother brought him to school every morning and waited for him every afternoon, in the Tuttons' black Packard.

Coming and going, just inside the front door of school, he was ambushed.

Ella Gwen charged to the rescue, pulling boys' hair, kicking their shins, causing enough commotion to summon the teachers from their classrooms and give Nelson time to escape.

Then there was Carrie Speck, freshman year, with bulbous acne, the victim of the girls.

"If you squeeze Carrie," one of them became famous for saying, "pus will come out."

Carrie was invited by Ella Gwen to come along to Murray's with us. Ella Gwen passed her the only notes she got in classes, and sat with her in school assemblies, and got her to join us in the bleachers at games.

Ella Gwen was a rescuer of losers and a bringer home of stray cats and dogs, so sentimental she cried when Eddie Cantor sang his closing song nights on the radio: "I love to spend each Wednesday with you. . . ."

She also spent as much time as I did in the town library, after school. The librarians, already in their coats, would have to dig us out of the stacks at closing time.

Ella Gwen could always find "the good parts" in novels, and she loved what she called "real love poetry." Not Elizabeth Barrett Browning, with her timid

How do I love thee? Let me count the ways,

but Oscar Wilde with

> *For all night long he murmured honeyed words,*
> *And saw her sweet unravished limbs, and kissed*
> *Her pale and argent body undisturbed,*
> *And paddled with the polished throat and pressed*
> *His hot and beating heart upon her chill and icy breast.*

Hyman Ginzburg was the third after-school library addict in our town.

He was almost eighteen. A tall, thin-haired Jewish refugee from Nazi Germany, he wore little gold-rimmed eyeglasses, talked with an accent, collected stamps, and played both violin and piano. He spoke three languages and used "big words" in English.

He was as strange in our small upstate New York town as anyone would be who'd landed from Mars on a spaceship. We didn't have that many Jews in town. People like my father weren't even sure "Jew" was what you could politely call one, and insisted on describing one as "a person of the Jewish persuasion."

No one in our town had ever had the name Hyman. The word itself was never spoken, unless you were talking privately about the wedding night.

Hyman Ginzburg made everything all the worse for himself by refusing all invitations to go out for basketball. He was six foot four.

He said he didn't care for sports.

When they weren't calling him "a queer," they were calling

him "Hyman the Hopeless"; "Hopeless" for short.

They felt he really was.

It happened on an ordinary winter afternoon in the library.

I had just "discovered" Thomas Wolfe. I had found a book by him in the stacks, and opened it to

For you are what you are, you know what you know, and there are no words for loneliness, black, bitter, aching loneliness, that gnaws the roots of silence in the night.

Around the same time I would sit by our phonograph at home, singing along with Frank Sinatra's record of "All or Nothing at All," playing it over and over.

My father would ask me, "What do you mean, half a love doesn't appeal to you?"

You don't have to answer that kind of a question from a father . . . but I don't know how I would have answered it even to myself. I, who was going steady with Donald Dare one fast kiss at the door and *pfffft*, with " 'Murder' He Says" for a love song?

I don't know what I thought I knew about black, bitter, aching loneliness gnawing, either . . . but I was hugging Wolfe to me, rushing through the stacks of the library, to find Ella Gwen and show the passage to her.

In between the volumes of Louisa May Alcott and James Joyce, they were standing. It was late afternoon, and the sun was coming through an upper window, fixing them in a dagger of light.

The first thing I thought was that Hyman looked like a

ninny. He had bad posture anyway, and he was stooped over, with his long neck hanging out like a chicken's, the gold-rimmed glasses slipping down his long, crooked nose. He had this deeply dizzy smile on his face. He looked like he'd gone quietly mad.

Ella Gwen wasn't faring well, either. She was gazing up at him with a stunned expression, as though someone had just thrown a rock at the back of her head. Her mouth hung open. She had wide, frightened, Bambi eyes.

The two of them looked like a cartoon, until Hyman suddenly leaned forward and put his mouth gently against hers.

I had never seen that anywhere but in the movies, while I was eating Butterfingers and Tootsie Rolls, giggling and elbowing the girls on both sides of me.

It was a long, long kiss, but in a few short seconds they had outdistanced me.

I was left far behind, to date a boy with dead people in his downstairs, who didn't even French kiss.

It was not just what I saw, either, there in the row of books from A to J. It was what I felt, an electricity they had and I had never had. They were wired for sound, and I was not even plugged in.

I plodded through the stacks toward the front of the library, trying to remember all the other times the three of us were there. How had they gotten from then to where they were without my knowing it?

"Oh, you're checking out my old pal Thomas Wolfe!" the librarian exclaimed. "I remember how *I* felt when I first read him. I still love *You Can't Go Home Again*!"

That was the last thing I wanted to hear.

She was an old maid who lived by herself in one room, at a place called The Women's Union. She went to all the band concerts in Hoopes Park on Saturday nights in summer, with another old maid who taught second grade. Some evenings she ate alone in the window of Weddigen's Restaurant on Genesee Street.

"Enjoy it, Marijane!"

I wished she wouldn't sing my name out like we knew each other that well, or had anything in common.

———

In high school we watched the ones in love more than we watched the ones who scored touchdowns, made baskets, had the leads in school plays, sang at assemblies, or called out all the funny lines that disrupted classes and got sent to the principal's office.

The ones in love were always on. You didn't have to wait until a special day to see them, or go anyplace to find them, or do anything or pay anything for the privilege of watching them.

They were always there.

They were different from us.

We were Jane and Robert and Tom and Marilyn and Eddie, but they were JohnandJan, LarryandGloria, BillandDeenie.

They were even different from those of us who went steady like they did. We had the name without the game. We were sheep going through the motions of the herd. They were in the grip of something that sent them on long walks by themselves down behind the stadium during lunch hours, and kept them lingering by lockers long after the bell for class rang.

We were ascending, even our voices were still childishly high as we called out to each other. They were falling in love, descending, and their tones were low and sensual. No dances in the gym were really underway until they got there. No dancers danced quite the same way they did together.

News of anything Hitler, Roosevelt, or Churchill did took second place to news of any of their breakups. They were The Ones.

Of all the lovers in our small town, in 1943, HymanandEllaGwen were The Golden Ones.

A Jewish leper would have been more welcome in Hyman's house than Ella Gwen was. She was a *shiksa*—from the Hebrew *sheques*, meaning "blemish." The Ginzburgs were Orthodox Jews. Ella Gwen was pork, bacon, ham, oysters, and shrimp. She was a *goy*, as in the sentence *Dos ken nor a goy*: "*That*, only a *goy* is capable of doing!"

Dr. Logan had only to hear that Ella Gwen "admired" someone in her class with the name Hyman Ginzburg. The mere mention of that name was enough to transform him into a raving madman, threatening to pack her off to boarding school or send her to St. Louis to live with her grandparents.

Hopeless Hyman, "the queer," became a new, dark, romantic hero, and basketball was, after all, a "boys' " game.

JohnandJan, LarryandGloria, and BillandDeenie paled before HymanandEllaGwen.

When we watched HymanandEllaGwen, we watched a love affair that Shakespeare, MGM, or Cole Porter couldn't have made more passionate and doomed.

They were our own Tristram and Iseult, Romeo and Juliet, Héloise and Abelard.

We watched them as you'd watch someone young and dying, or something splendid on its way to ruin.

Dear M.J.,

Can Hy call you when he wants to get in touch with me? You must never, never, never let anyone in your family know you're our go-between if you agree. I know it's a lot to ask, but you're the only one I can trust. We are so in love it hurts! Have you read This Is My Beloved? Hy gave me a copy. Our song is "You'll Never Know." He is such a doll! It is worth all the sneaking around we have to do. It is worth everything in this world! Please let me know if we can count on you! We were at Hunter's Point yesterday afternoon. It is our place. Oh Gawd, it was beautiful! Love ya. EGL

Dear Ella Gwen,

Hy can always call me. You can count on me. Natch! Where do I get This Is My Beloved? It's not in the library. Have you gone all the way? Don't answer that if you don't want to. Love ya. MJ

Dear M.J.,

Here is my copy of This Is My Beloved. You'll see why it's not in the library. Read the underlined parts first.

I told Hy if it would help I would even become Jewish. I honestly mean that! He told his father I

said it, and his father said saying a broche over a chicken won't make it a fish. He said a female gentile can't become a Jew since she has the children and she must be born a Jew. (A broche is Jewish for blessing.) So we are really up a creek without a paddle, since the Ginzburgs are as bad as my own family when it comes to Hy and me. We are getting desperate since he is eighteen now and will be drafted soon. He'll call you tonight to say when and where I should meet him. I'm saying I'm going to the Red Cross to roll bandages with you. We will never never forget what you are doing for us. Love ya. EGL
P.S. I almost faint after we kiss for a long time and Hy says he feels like a firecracker that has to go off. Never, never repeat any of this!

Dear Ella Gwen,

Thanks for the book. I'll read it late tonight. Don't say you're rolling bandages with me. Say you're going to see For Whom the Bell Tolls, which is where Donald and I are going. You know the plot already from the book by Ernest Hemingway, so you're safe if your folks grill you. Love ya. MJ
P.S. Have you gone all the way?

Dear M.J.,

I got my first 70 ever (in English) in all my life! My father is furious! He says he wonders what my mind's on when I'm doing my homework. (If he knew he'd croak!) I can't go out week nights anymore. Hy and I are skipping school Tuesday and going some-

place in his father's car. Neither of us cares what happens anymore, except he'll have to go to war and then what'll we do? I have never, never, never felt this way about anyone or thought anyone could about anyone. Love ya. EGL
P.S. Almost.

One afternoon when I arrived home from school, I knew I was in big trouble.

My mother was waiting for me in the hall.

She was carrying something in her hand, behind her back. One of the afternoon soap operas was playing in the living room, through the Stromberg-Carlson. She had walked away from it for this encounter. There was a brand-new V-letter from my brother in the silver tray on the hall table, but she wasn't pointing it out to me.

"What is this?" She whipped out the copy of *This Is My Beloved* and held it up to my face, the same way she'd thrust a turd in a paper towel at Skippy's nose when we were housebreaking him.

"It's a book," I said.

"I know it's a book!"

"It's poetry."

"It's filth!"

"I wouldn't call it filth."

"What would you call it?" She was opening it with shaking hands, until she came to

We need so little room, we two . . .
thus on a single pillow, as we move
nearer, nearer Heaven . . .

"Nearer, nearer Heaven" was gasped out, but her voice gained a certain outraged momentum as she spat out the last nine words:

until I burst inside you like a screaming rocket!

I couldn't think of anything to say. She was fighting to get her breath back.

"Just *one* of the underlined parts," said my mother. "One of the *few* underlined parts I can even read aloud!"

"I didn't underline them."

"Ella Gwen Logan underlined them!"

"Okay," I said.

"Oh, no, it is *not* okay," she said. "I don't want this kind of trash in this house! I don't want you reading this kind of trash!"

"All it's about is people in love," I said.

"Is that what Ella Gwen Logan says it's about?"

"She doesn't have to. I can read."

"I don't want you to see Ella Gwen Logan anymore."

"Then I'll have to wear a blindfold to school."

"This is *not* a joke!"

From the living room, a woman's voice was delivering the Bell Telephone commercial:

Give him a break. Evening is about his only chance to tele-phone home. He can get through easier if the wires aren't crowded—and his call means so much to him and the home folks. . . . So please, don't call long distance between—

My mother was concluding a minilecture on Ella Gwen's history of calling my attention to obscene literature with ". . . and you are not to take any more calls from Hyman Ginzburg! Tell him not to call here again! I know what's going on!"

"You've been going through my desk again!"

"Everyone in this town knows what's going on. The Logans are the last to know what's going on right under their noses!"

"A person's desk is supposed to be private property."

"A person's desk is not supposed to be filled with secret plans that help Ella Gwen Logan go off to Hunter's Point, to neck and pet, et cetera, with an older boy her parents don't approve of!"

"They don't et cetera, and you know *why* the Logans hate Hy! The Logans are prejudiced!"

"That's the Logans' business. I don't have anything against Hyman Ginzburg per se, but I do have plenty against what the two of them are up to!"

"Why isn't that the two of them's business?"

"Because they're making it your business, that's why. Because they're making you a party to what they're doing in the woods and in cars, and you tell her you're forbidden to have anything more to do with her!"

"She's my best friend."

"She *was* your best friend."

"She still is, whether I have anything to do with her or not."

"Then enjoy your memories of Ella Gwen Logan, because she is not to come here, or to call here, and you are not to go there, or call there, and Hyman Ginzburg is not to call here. She's a bad influence on you!"

"All she did wrong was fall in love," I complained.

"All she did wrong," said my mother, slapping the thin book down hard on the hall table, "is let her feelings for that boy get way out of hand!" She marched herself back into the living room. "*Way* out of hand!" she called over her shoulder.

Back to that hot August night of my date with Donald Dare.

As we go down my front walk, I whisper to him, "Did you get it?"

"It's parked down on Marvin Avenue."

"The hearse or the flower car?"

"The flower car."

"You didn't park it in front of the McIntees', did you? If Mrs. McIntee sees me getting into the flower car with you, she'll call my mother just as sure as the sun'll come up tomorrow!"

"I parked it way down past old man Palmer's house."

We're holding hands as we walk along. Across the street, Mr. and Mrs. Hunter are sitting side by side in wicker rockers on their front porch, smiling at us, waving. Behind them, in their window, there's a gold star hanging. Their son, Hooton, went down with the USS *Oklahoma* when the Japs torpedoed

it at Pearl Harbor. . . . Next to their house, in the De Marcos'
window, are three blue stars for Nick, Sam, and Tony De
Marco, all Marines now.

We are considered the street lovers. Neighbors out hosing
their Victory gardens or reading the evening paper on their
porches brighten at the sight of us, enjoying the idea Donald
and I are off to a movie and Murray's—young lovers still
young enough not to be touched by the war.

The Dares' flower car looks like a long limousine with the
back cut out, leaving an open space. It is the show-flower
car, the one that follows the hearse to the cemetery, with
eighty percent of all the floral tributes. There is a smaller
flower car, a station wagon, rushed to the cemetery ahead of
the hearse, with the other twenty percent, so the grave has
some decorations around it when the mourners arrive.

The show-flower car has a C sticker on its windshield, meaning it qualifies for extra gas since it's needed for an essential
business activity.

The only thing in the open space tonight is Hyman Glitz-
burg's duffel bag.

Hyman is waiting in the front seat of the flower car. Perspira-
tion runs down his face, making it hard for him to keep his
glasses on his nose, and he's giving his wristwatch nervous
glances.

The three of us are squeezed into the front seat.

"Walking out the front door was hard," Hyman says. "My
father said, 'Well, it's Shabbos, but it's your last night, too,
and it's still Shabbos tomorrow when we put you on your

train. So say good-bye to your friends.' "

Hyman has orders to report to Fort Knox, Kentucky.

As we ride downtown, Spike Jones' band comes over the radio:

Ven der Fuehrer says
"Ve iss der Master race,"
Ve heil (phhht!)
Heil (phffft!)
Right in der Fuehrer's face!

"Over here they think Adolph Hitler's funny," Hy says.

"It's that mustache," Donald says.

Ella Gwen is waiting for us behind The Women's Union, where she has told her family she was going to roll bandages for the Red Cross. She's wearing a yellow jumper the color of her hair, a white blouse, and brown-and-white spectator pumps.

She has managed to carry a shoulder bag and a knitting bag out of her house, crammed with extra underwear, a dress, a nightie, shoes, a cardigan, and blue jeans.

She tells us about it after she climbs in front, where she has to sit on Hyman's lap.

We are in for an hour-and-a-half ride to Syracuse, New York.

As we drive out of town, we're all perspiring in the hot night and singing along with the radio:

Don't sit under the apple tree
With anyone else but me . . .

It is still light out, and we go over the big hills, past the lush farmlands, and into the little town of Skaneateles, known for having the coldest of all the Finger Lakes. It is the first thing we see, a slim streak of bright-blue water, with a long green lawn in front of it. A band concert is in full swing there, while out on the lake boats are letting down their sails at buoys. There are soldiers and sailors strolling near the bandstand with girls, and old people wiping their necks with handkerchiefs, sitting on benches, listening to "The Battle Hymn of the Republic."

Summers past, our families would bring us to this town to eat at The Krebs, a famous restaurant, and to attend The Skaneateles Summer Theater, where "real" actors and actresses performed in plays like *Our Town*.

We go on our way, along familiar roads, through hill-circled hamlets, past Holsteins heading in toward red barns, pointing out the sunset sinking in the treetops behind us. We see the first star of the evening in the slate-blue sky, and we make lots of nervous little jokes about what's going to happen when "they" finally find the notes left for them.

"My father is going to have a conniption fit!" Ella Gwen says.

"Mine's going to say Kaddish!"—Hy.

When we get to the Syracuse station, we lose some of the high sense of adventure. We push our way through the thronged terminal beneath big signs begging everyone to travel light. We trip over suitcases, bags, boxes, packages, and rope-tied bundles, while Hy rushes ahead for the tickets. We stand under a huge sign warning:

A SLIP OF THE LIP WILL SINK A SHIP!

Ella Gwen keeps thanking Donald and me and watching for Hy. Young men in white and khaki uniforms not much older than we all are, are locked in embraces with their girls, their mothers, sisters, and grandmothers. A loudspeaker blares, announcing train arrivals and departures.

Suddenly Hy is running toward us crying, "Track nine. That's us! Hurry, honey!"

Ella Gwen reaches up to hug me, tears starting in her blue eyes. I hate myself for hearing the echo of my mother's voice, just for a second, "*Way* out of hand!"

Kisses and promises to write, then Ella Gwen runs with Hy, almost losing one of her spectator pumps, which falls off her bare foot. She gets it back on; Hy's arm slips around her waist, they look back at us, laughing.

One more time before they disappear up the tunnel leading to the trains, they stop a second to wave good-bye. We can't see Ella Gwen through the onrushing crowd, only Hy, because he's so tall. He's wrinkled up his nose, mouthing the word "good-bye," looking like someone grimacing from a stab wound.

Then they are gone.

On the way back, Donald and I don't talk a lot. I ride way over on the seat next to him. I can smell the Vitalis he puts on his hair.

We pass Burma Shave signs along the roadside, glimpsing their messages in the headlights.

There are usually six in a row, saying things like:

> Hardly a driver
> Is now alive
> Who passes
> On hills
> At 75
> Burma Shave

For the first time, I realize the war has changed them, too. Donald reads them aloud as we go by.

> Let's make Hitler
> and Hirohito
> Look as sick
> As Benito
> Buy Defense Bonds
> Burma Shave

We sit very close, for us, listening to music, songs about missing the one you love, waiting for the one you love, coming home to the one you love. In my mind's eye I see Hy towering over my little best friend, his long arm reaching down around her waist, and the glint of his eyeglasses as they looked back laughing, her small hand blowing a kiss, the heavy knitting bag with her things in it on her arm.

At one point I say, "Their song was 'You'll Never Know.' " They are already in the past tense.

Donald says, "Well, they made it. They got out."

When we finally get to Marvin Avenue, where we'll leave the flower car, Donald says, "Okay, we saw *The More the Merrier* tonight. With Jean Arthur and Joel McCrea. My mother saw it last night, and I know all you need to know if you're cross-examined. . . . It's about a Washington government girl who—"

While he runs through the plot for me, I watch his face in profile. I toy with the idea of terrifying him into speechlessness by saying right out, "I love you, Donald Dare, and this has been the best evening of my entire life!"

"Did you get all that?" he asks me.

"I got it. I'll walk in the house and say, 'Am I glad I'm not one of those poor girls who has to work for the government in Washington!' "

Donald imitates my mother's voice. "Why do you say that, dear?"

"She never calls me dear."

"Why do you say that, Marijane?"

"Well, poor Jean Arthur rented her half to this daffy old man—"

"Her half of what?"

"Her half of her four-room apartment in Washington, D.C. You know, Mother, apartments are impossible to get in big cities like Washington."

"Which is why you should thank your lucky stars you're living here with Daddy and me, darling."

I give his arm a punch. "She'd *never* call me darling!"

We're starting to laugh hysterically when Donald says, "It's seven to twelve. We're just going to make it!" He opens the door to the flower car.

We race through the vacant lot up from Marvin Avenue toward my house.

At the door we're out of breath.

We always had this corny little routine before the good-night kiss. It went:

I'll give you a ring—Donald.

What kind?—me.

Diamond.

Tonight he just says, "I'll call you tomorrow."

He kisses me. There is just the slightest flicker of his tongue against my lips, too slight to be *le baiser Français*, but we are certainly moving nearer, nearer Heaven, though at a snail's pace.

As Donald runs down our front walk, he stops halfway and jumps in the air, clicking his heels together.

"What's he running for?" my father says as I come through the front door.

The mantel clock is bonging twelve times.

"What where you spying at us through the venetian blinds for?"

"What's Famine's big hurry? Did someone die?" my father says.

"Was the movie good?" my mother asks.

"Am I glad I'm not one of those poor girls who has to work for the government in Washington, D.C.," I begin, walking into our living room.

Behind me, my father says, "The government's glad you're not, too."

———————

En route to Fort Knox, Kentucky, EllaGwenandHyman stopped over in Elkton, Maryland, where Ella Gwen presented her birth certificate to a judge, the year 1927 changed to 1925.

About a year later, Private First Class Hyman Ginzburg became the father of a boy they named Donald, for Seaman Recruit Donald Dare.

. . . I was home last week for mom's funeral [Ella Gwen wrote in one letter from Leesville, Louisiana]. *Daddy hardly looked at Donnie or spoke to me, and Hy's folks didn't even want to talk on the phone, so nothing's changed that way. Your mom was real nice to me, making a fuss over Donnie and stuff. She says you love boarding school. I guess anything to get out of that town! I don't ever want to go back there, even though this little town is no picnic. But we're all together, the three of us, so I can't complain. Love ya. EGG*
P.S. Have you gone all the way?

After the war I lost track of Ella Gwen and Hyman. None of her family are living anymore, and Hy's family moved away from our town.

While I never wrote a book about Ella Gwen and Hy, I modeled a character after Hy in a book called *If I Love You, Am I Trapped Forever?*

Hy became Duncan Stein, nicknamed "Doomed" by the high school kids in the fictional upstate New York town I always call Cayuta.

I borrowed some of Donald Dare, too, for a book I called *I'll*

Love You When You're More Like Me. I called him Wally Wither-spoon, and I moved his family to Long Island, New York. I also borrowed Gorilla, their cat, who liked to sleep with "guests."

Fact is always stranger than fiction.

In the late sixties I visited my hometown, and driving in, I saw a sign reading:

DRIVE CAREFULLY
<u>WE CAN WAIT</u>
DARE & SON, FUNERAL DIRECTORS

The last time I saw Donald, he was standing at a party, holding a scotch and soda, smoking a pipe, and rocking on his heels contentedly while he listened to me describe memories of us.

"I can't remember not wanting to be a funeral director," he said. "Are you sure that's not just your writer's imagination?"

I said I was sure.

"I enjoy what I do," Donald said. "Good money, and you work at home."

"In the shop," I said.

"That's right." He smiled.

"But I do remember our trip to Syracuse in the flower car," Donald said. "My namesake would be about twenty-eight now."

"That was one of our finer moments," I said.

"How do you know?" Donald said. "Maybe they didn't even stay together. Not many around here have who got married during the war." He took his pipe out of his mouth to punctuate what he'd say next. "War or no war, if I'd have been Doc Logan, I'd have tracked her down and kicked his ass! My own daughter tried to run off with a hippie a while back, and I went out to

San Francisco and brought her home. . . . That was *my* finer moment."

My old pal Thomas Wolfe is wrong.

You *can* go home again.

You should.

It gives you lots to think about.

Two:
Where Are You Now, William Shakespeare?

My very first boyfriend was named William Shakespeare. This was his real name, and he lived over on Highland Hill, about a block from my house.

Billy Shakespeare didn't call at seven for dates, or suffer my father's inspection, or give me a silver identification bracelet. We didn't have a song, either.

I often went to his house to get him, or I met him down in the empty lot on Alden Avenue, or over at Hoopes Park, where we caught sunfish and brought them from the pond in bottles of murky water with polliwogs.

Marijane is ten [my father wrote in his journal]. *She plays with boys and looks like one.*

This was true.

My arms and knees were full of scabs from falls out of trees and off my bicycle. I was happiest wearing the pants my brother'd grown out of, the vest to one of my father's business suits over one of my brother's old shirts, Indian moccasins, and a cap. Everything I said came out of the side of my mouth, and I strolled around with my fists inside my trouser pockets.

This did not faze Billy Shakespeare, whose eyes lit up when he saw me coming, and who readily agreed that when we married we'd name our first son Ellis, after my father, and not William after him.

"Because William Shakespeare is a funny name," I'd say.

"It isn't funny. It's just that there's a famous writer with the same name," he'd say.

"Do you agree to Ellis Shakespeare then?"

"Sure, if it's all right with your father."

"He'll be pleased," I'd tell Billy.

Around this time, I was always trying to think of ways to please my father. (The simplest way would have been to wear a dress and a big hair ribbon, stay out of trees, stop talking out of the side of my mouth, and act like a girl . . . but I couldn't have endured such misery even for him.)

Billy Shakespeare accepted the fact, early in our relationship, that my father was my hero. He protested only slightly when I insisted that the reason my father wasn't President of the United States was that my father didn't want to be.

That was what my father told me, when I'd ask him why he wasn't President. I'd look at him across the table at dinner, and think, He knows more than anybody knows, he's handsome, and he always gets things done—so he ought to be President. If he was, I'd think, there'd be no problems in the world.

Sometimes I'd ask him: "Daddy, why aren't you President of the United States?"

His answer was always the same.

"I wouldn't want that job for anything. We couldn't take a walk without Secret Service men following us. Do you think we could go up to the lake for a swim by ourselves? No. There'd be Secret Service men tagging along. It'd ruin our lives. It'd end our privacy. Would you want that?"

Billy Shakespeare would say, "He's not President because nobody elected him President."

"He won't let anyone elect him," I'd answer. "He doesn't want Secret Service men around all the time."

"I'm not sure he could *get* elected," Billy would venture.

"He could get elected," I'd tell Billy. "He doesn't want to! We like our privacy!"

"Okay." Billy'd give in a little. "But he never tried getting elected, so he really doesn't know if he could."

I'd wave that idea away with my dirty hands. "Don't worry. He'd be elected in a minute if he wanted to be. You don't know *him.*"

Billy Shakespeare's other rivals for my attention were movie stars. I'd write Clark Gable and Henry Fonda and Errol Flynn, and they'd send back glossy photos of themselves and sometimes letters, too.

These photographs and letters were thumbtacked to the

fiberboard walls of a playhouse my father'd had built for me in our backyard.

When I did play with a girl, the game was always the same: getting dinner ready for our husbands. I had an old set of dishes back in the playhouse, and my girl friend and I played setting the table for dinner. During this game, Billy Shakespeare was forgotten. When my husband came through the playhouse door, he would be one of the movie stars pinned to the wall.

I played this game with Dorothy Spencer, who lived behind our house.

She was a tall redhead who looked like a girl, and who always had it in her head to fix meat loaf with mashed potatoes for a movie star named Spencer Tracy.

I changed around a lot—the menu as well as the movie star—but Dorothy stuck to meat loaf with mashed for Spencer.

I'd be saying, "Well, Clark is a little late tonight and the turkey is going to be overdone," or "Gee, Henry isn't here yet and the ham is going to be dried up." But Dorothy would persist with "Spencer's going to love this meat loaf when he gets here. I'll wait until I hear his footsteps to mash the potatoes."

Billy Shakespeare was jealous of this game and tried his best to ruin it with reality.

He'd say, "What are two famous movie stars doing living in the same house?"

He'd say, "How come famous movie stars only have a one-room house with no kitchen?"

But Dorothy Spencer and I went on happily playing house,

until the movie *Brother Rat* came to town.

That was when we both fell in love with the movie star Ronald Reagan.

Suddenly we were both setting the table for the same movie star—different menus, but the same husband.

"You've always stuck to meat loaf and mashed for Spencer!" I said angrily. "Now you want my Ronald!"

"He's not *your* Ronald," she said.

"It's my playhouse, though," I reminded her.

"But I won't play if I can't have Ronald," she said

"We both can't have Ronald!" I insisted.

We took the argument to her mother, who told us to pretend Ronald Reagan was twins. Then we could both have him.

"He isn't twins, though," Dorothy said.

"And if he is," I put in, "I want the real Ronald, and not his twin."

Our game came to a halt, but our rivalry did not. Both of us had written to Ronald Reagan and were waiting for his reply.

"No matter what he writes her," I told Billy Shakespeare, "my letter from him will be better."

"You might not even get a letter," Billy said. "She might not get one either."

"She might not get one," I said, "but I will."

"You don't know that," Billy said.

"Do you want to know why I know I'll get one?" I asked him.

I made him cross his heart and hope to die if he told anyone what I'd done.

Billy was a skinny little kid with big eyes that always got bigger when I was about to confess to him something I'd done.

"Crossmyheartandhopetodie," he said very fast. "What'd you do?"

"You know that Ronald Reagan isn't like any of the others," I said.

"Because Dorothy Spencer likes him, too."

"That's got nothing to do with it!" I said. "He's just different. I never felt this way about another movie star."

"Why?"

"*Why?* I don't know why! That's the way love is."

"Love?" Billy said.

"Yes. What did you think made me write him that I was a crippled child, and had to go to see him in a wheelchair?"

"Oh migosh!" Billy exclaimed. "Oh migosh!"

"I had to get his attention somehow."

"Oh migosh!"

"Just shut up about it!" I warned him. "If word gets out I'll know it's you."

Dorothy Spencer was the first to hear from Ronald Reagan. She didn't get a letter, but she got a signed photograph.

"Since I heard from him first," she said, "he's my husband."

"Not in my playhouse!" I said.

"He wrote me back first," she said.

"Just wait," I said.

"I don't have to wait," she said. "I'm setting the table for him in my own house."

"It's not even your house, it's your father's," I said. "At

least when he's married to me, we'll have our own house."

"He's married to me now," she said.

"We'll see about that," I said.

I was beginning to get a panicky feeling as time passed and no mail came from Ronald Reagan. You'd think he'd write back to a crippled child first. . . . Meanwhile Dorothy was fixing him meat loaf and mashed at her place.

I had pictures of him cut out of movie magazines scotch-taped to my bedroom walls. I went to sleep thinking about him, wondering why he didn't care enough to answer me.

The letter and photograph from Ronald Reagan arrived on a Saturday.

I saw the Hollywood postmark and let out a whoop, thereby attracting my father's attention.

"What's all the excitement?"

I was getting the photograph out of the envelope. "I got a picture from Ronald Reagan!"

"Who's he?"

"Some movie star," my mother said.

By that time I had the photograph out. My heart began to beat nervously as I read the inscription at the bottom. "To a brave little girl, in admiration, Ronald Reagan."

"What does it say?" my father said.

"Nothing, it's just signed," I said, but he already saw what it said as he stood behind me looking down at it.

"Why are you a brave little girl?" he asked.

"How do I know?" I said.

"There's a letter on the floor," said my mother.

"That's my letter," I said, grabbing it.

"Why are you considered a brave little girl?" my father again. "Why does *he* admire *you*?"

I held the letter to my chest. "Those are just things they say," I said.

"They say you're *brave*?" my father said.

"Brave or honest or any dumb thing," I said weakly.

"Read the letter, Marijane," said my father.

I read the letter to myself.

> *Dear Marijane,*
> *Thank you for your letter.*
> *Remember that a handicap can be a challenge.*
> *Always stay as cheerful as you are now.*
> *Yours truly,*
> *Ronald Reagan*

"What does it say?" my mother asked.

"Just the usual," I said. "They never say much."

"Let me see it, brave little girl," my father said.

"It's to me."

"Marijane . . ." and he had his hand out.

After my father read the letter, and got the truth out of me concerning my correspondence with Ronald Reagan, he told me what I was to do.

What I was to do was to sit down immediately and write Ronald Reagan, telling him I had lied. I was to add that I thanked God for my good health. I was to return both the letter and the photograph.

No Saturday in my entire life had ever been so dark.

My father stood over me while I wrote the letter in tears,

convinced that Ronald Reagan would hate me all his life for my deception. I watched through blurred eyes while my father took my letter, Ronald Reagan's letter, and the signed photograph, put them into a manila envelope, addressed it, sealed it, and put it in his briefcase to take to the post office.

For weeks and weeks after that, I dreaded the arrival of our postman. I was convinced a letter'd come beginning,

> *Dear Marijane,*
> *How very disappointed I am in you. . . .*

"I don't think he'll write back," Billy Shakespeare told me. "I don't think he'll want anything more to do with you."

That ended getting dinner for movie stars in my playhouse. I told Dorothy Spencer that I'd outgrown all that.

Three years after I wrote Ronald Reagan that letter, I slumped way down in my seat in humiliation as I watched him lose a leg in the movie *King's Row.* . . . I was sure he thought of the little liar from upstate New York who'd pretended she was crippled.

Many, many years later, the man I always thought should be President of the United States was dead, and Ronald Reagan was President of the United States.

I didn't vote for him.

I heard Dorothy Spencer got married, and I envision her making meat loaf and mashed for her husband.

The only remaining question is, Where are you now, William Shakespeare?

Three:
Marijane the Spy

You were different-looking. Definitely. Maybe if you hadn't been, you'd have fared better in our small town, but I doubt it, because you were also terrified of all of us, of everything, and we knew it.

You were the opposite of me, a very girly girl. You had on little white gloves, and a hat and anklets, and shiny patent-leather shoes, and you were very careful about your dress, smoothing it across your knees as you sat, so it wouldn't wrinkle.

Remember, I was the first one from the town to speak to you? The way I spoke to anyone my own age, about to enter my town via bus from Syracuse, was to ask questions.

"Well, how long are you staying?"

"I don't know."

"How come you don't know?"

"Because it's up to my mother."

"But you have to go to school, don't you?"

"I don't know."

"But you probably will, won't you?"

"I said I didn't know."

"Where did you go to school before?"

"In New York."

"In New York City?"

"Yes."

"Do you live in New York City?"

"I did."

"How come you left there for here?"

"My mother wanted to."

"Where is she?"

"She's coming."

"What is she going to do here?"

"I don't know."

"You don't seem to know much about your own life."

Silence.

I was on my way back from an afternoon at the orthodontist. I was eleven. I took the bus thirty-six miles for this bimonthly appointment with the dentist on Salina Street, in Syracuse.

I hated my braces, but I liked the bus rides. There were often prisoners on the bus, because of the state prison in our town. They'd be aboard coming and going. Going they carried birdcages, sometimes, with the only pets they were allowed to have perched inside them, and going they wore shiny dark suits the state issued them.

Coming, they were handcuffed to other men, slouched in their seats, getting their last glimpses of freedom before their sentences began.

Young girls, alone, weren't often on the bus, and when they were I usually knew them. There was Kathy Gates, who took the bus to see her grandmother in Syracuse. There was Ida Leonard, who wore an earphone and saw a doctor there. There were girls from a crowd a few years older than I was who went to shop at Flah's and Addises' and Dey Brothers.

You were a stranger on your way to my town, and I was bent on investigating you. As a younger kid, I'd played spy and organized a gang to go and look in windows and report back everything they saw in our neighborhood.

My older brother'd hung a sign on my bedroom door,

MARIJANE THE SPY

My mother was a great gossip, and I listened to everything she said on the telephone to her friends. Saturday nights the two of us would drive downtown and park on Genesee Street and just watch: who went to the movies with who, who went into Boyson's Restaurant with who, who went into the liquor store for a bottle, on and on.

My father knew how my mother loved all this sort of thing, and his favorite greeting to her when he came through the front door every night was "Any news? Any gossip? Any scandal?"

You were mysterious, I felt. You didn't give good answers

to all my questions. You were somehow overly proper in your mannerisms, very very pale, with this long black hair and frightened big brown eyes, and you looked like a little old lady in a young body.

I looked funny myself. I always did. I had on a dress with my father's business-suit vest over it, an old red turban of my mother's on my head, and saddle shoes with white wool gym socks. I was androgynous. My father's journal read: *Marijane, at 11, is neither boy nor girl but somewhere in between, with braces on her teeth now so she won't smile—in a stage of answering her mother back. Not me yet.*

(Not *him* yet was a joke. One answer back to him and *pow!* He was the violent type, not at all above taking his kids down to the basement for a real beating with a length of rope. Battered kids hadn't been invented yet by the psychiatrists, but we were there, unnamed but bruised—and often badly. My father had this dark side to him, and many a dinner hour was disrupted by trips down to the cellar, after he'd listened to my mother's recital of things we kids had done that day. . . . No, we didn't answer *him* back!)

You looked more like a kid who got beat up in the basement than I did. You looked as though you had many bad secrets.

I told you my name. I told you my father owned Ivanhoe Foods.

"My grandfather," I said, "owns most of the grocery stores in town. He has a monopoly."

I don't know where I even got that word, but it didn't seem to impress you.

You stayed unchanged, smoothing your dress with your gloved hands, staring straight ahead.

"So what's your name?"

"Millicent."

"Milly?"

"Millicent."

"Millicent what?"

"It doesn't matter."

"Millicent It Doesn't Matter?"

You didn't think that was funny.

You were looking out at the hills and the green farmlands. People said our part of upstate New York looked like Switzerland, with a lake over every hill, and meadows with wild flowers, the bluest skies and whitest clouds.

"What's it like in New York?"

"It's crowded."

"Is it dirty?"

"Some parts are."

"Where did you live?"

"A Hundred and Ninth Street."

"Is that near Radio City Music Hall?"

"No."

"I was there. I was at Radio City Music Hall."

"I wasn't."

"I was. One Easter."

No comment, and in a little while you fell asleep or pretended to, probably the latter, so you wouldn't have to talk to me.

When the bus finally pulled into the depot, I was surprised to see Mrs. Burnside there to greet you.

She was Nancy Burnside's mother, and she ran one of the many tourist homes we had in town. Nancy's father had disappeared when she was very little, and her mother supported the family by taking in lodgers.

"Hi, Mrs. Burnside," I said, hanging around a little after we got off the bus, ignoring my mother waiting across the street in her car. "I've been talking with Millicent here, but she doesn't seem to know if she's going to school with us."

"You run along, Marijane" was what Mrs. Burnside said.

"I was just trying to be friendly," I said, and Mrs. Burnside, who had my number, said again to "just run along, dear."

I said good-bye to you, and you acknowledged it with a slight nod of your head.

"There was this strange girl on the bus named Millicent," I told my mother. "She's staying at Mrs. Burnside's, I guess."

"What's strange about her?" my mother said. "I saw her. She looks like a perfect little lady."

"That's what's strange," I said. "She is a little lady, but she's not much older than me."

"Make friends with her," my mother said. "Maybe some of it will rub off on you. Maybe you won't wear that vest everywhere."

"Maybe pigs will whistle," I said.

"Maybe I'll have to ask your father to talk to you about sassing me back," my mother said.

"He doesn't talk," I said, "the whip talks. 'Take that,' it says, 'and that!' "

"I hope you don't talk that way in school," my mother says.

"What way?"

"About the whip talking."

"Don't worry," I said, "your secret is safe. You're married to a man of violence but your secret is safe."

Your secret wasn't safe, not from the very moment I suspected you had one.

The next time I saw you was the very next day, when you arrived at Fulton School.

No seventh grader had ever showed up for school in a dress with a hat and gloves, nor worn patent-leather shoes on any day but Sunday.

Kindness is not an emotion natural to most preteens.

We looked you over good while you put your hat and gloves in your locker, and I filled everyone in on what I'd learned about you during the bus trip.

"She clams up when you ask her questions," I warned everyone.

"I'd hate to be new, and on a bus next to you with all your questions," said Ella Gwen Logan, living exception to the rule about kindness and preteens. "You probably scared her to death!"

"Something scared her," someone said, "because she looks like a ghost."

Then and there you became known as Miss Ghost. You were too prissy-looking to get by just as The Ghost.

I sallied forth to show off and greet you before the others.

"Hello, there, Millicent. We meet again. How do you like it over at the Burnsides'?"

"I don't know."

"Oh, here we go again with the I don't knows."

I was playing to the crowd.

I remember your hands, too, very white, with long elegant fingers and nails pointed and manicured with clear polish.

Most of us hadn't started growing our nails yet. What nails I had were there as excuses for my mother to yell at me to get a nail file, and get *all* the dirt out from under them.

"She's a nice girl," Ella Gwen Logan tried. "She's just a little formal."

"She's a snob," I said. "She's from New York City."

"What's she doing here?" someone asked.

"Try and find out," I said. "Miss Ghost isn't saying."

So it began for you, with me leading the pack. At every opportunity we tried to find out more about you, and you reacted by becoming almost totally silent. When lunch hour came you took your sandwiches down to the park at the corner, instead of to the cafeteria, and you dragged your feet as long as you could each day after school, so you could walk home by yourself, after we'd all left.

You finally stopped wearing the hat and gloves, and one day you appeared in new saddle shoes.

But nothing worked.

We dogged your footsteps, following you to the park, waiting until you came out of school afternoons after last class, asking you where you'd stashed your pretty bonnet and if you weren't afraid of germs with your gloves gone, and what made you give up your shiny shoes?

I got a brilliant idea that one day all the girls should show up for school in hats and gloves, and we did this, waltzing ourselves down to your park bench at noon, twirling around in front of you and saying things like "I just alighted from the bus from New York City, my dears, and I'm too too exhausted to talk!"

"How *do* you like my hat?"—another. "It's the latest fashion from New York City, where we do not talk to strangers ever!"

"Oh, New York City"—someone else. "You must be very, very rich!" .

"Not so rich that I can afford a hotel," it continued, "for I am presently ensconced at the Burnside Tourist Home."

Eventually, word got out that your mother was the new ticket taker at one of the local movie houses nights.

We all went by to get a look at her in her glass cage.

She was a tall, dark-haired woman, very thin, and as pale as you were, with her hair worn in a bun. We nicknamed her Mrs. Ghost, and went to the park at noon with new ammunition.

"I heard the Palace Theater went all the way to New York City to hire their new ticket taker!"

"Oh, I heard that, too, because, you know, a hick doesn't take the tickets like a city slicker does."

"You have to be very, very quicket to take a ticket!"

On and on it went.

One night Nancy Burnside telephoned me. She was in the older crowd, already a senior in high school.

"Marijane," she said, "I hear you kids have been giving Millicent a rough time. What's the story?"

"Did she tell you that?"

"Let up on her," said Nancy Burnside. "They're having a

rough time as it is, without you kids picking on her."

"Why are they having a rough time?"

"That isn't your business."

"We just wonder about her," I said. "She won't talk about herself."

"Why should she?"

"We talk about ourselves. Why doesn't she talk about herself?"

"Maybe she doesn't trust you yet."

"I don't trust anybody, but I still talk about myself," I said. "Why does somebody have to trust somebody to talk about herself?"

"Please, just give her a break. Okay?"

But my mother's ears picked up on the word "trust."

My mother said, "Of course, the Burnsides are always taking in people we don't know anything about, traveling salesmen and whatnot, but I've never known Pam Burnside to take in a mother and daughter. Seems peculiar that they don't rent a little place of their own, instead of living in one room down there."

She thought to add, "But I hope you girls aren't being cruel."

"We're just curious," I said.

"You know what that did to the cat," said my mother . . . and later I heard her on the telephone talking about the new boarders at the Burnsides'.

You were one of the brightest kids who ever passed through Fulton School. You had the highest grades in every subject, and the English teacher was always holding up something you wrote (with A+ at the top of it) as an example of neatness and good penmanship.

You never spoke in class unless you had to, never raised your hand and offered an answer, but you were regularly called on, and you always came up with the right answer.

Your clothes were always clean and neat, too, and the only time we ever saw you cry was when a boy sitting behind you tried to write Miss Ghost on the back of your dress with a pen.

You burst into tears and cried out, "My mother will never get that inkstain out!"

This did not daunt the demons of seventh grade one little bit.

We began to write "inkstain" on each other's shoulders, instantly forming "The Inkstain Sorority."

"Are you in Ink?" we'd ask each other.

We'd look over our shoulders at the writing there and reply, "I think I'm in Ink."

"Hey, Millicent," we'd call out, "are you in Ink?"

"I don't think she's in Ink," someone would answer. "Her mother would never get the inkstain out!"

"She's not in Ink, she's out!" we called out.

Somehow you lasted for six months before your secret was out.

I first got wind of it overhearing a conversation my mother was having with one of her friends, on the telephone.

"Why, I never even thought of that!" was all my mother had to say to make my ears perk up. "She takes in the relatives?

I'd be afraid to have them in my house."

I always counted on the fact my mother would be so caught up in new gossip that it would take her a while to perceive the danger of its being spread by what was huddled over in the chair behind her.

I would try not to even breathe so as not to remind her I was there.

"I never knew that about Pam Burnside," she continued. "But when you think about it, they have to stay someplace. I never even thought about why we had so many of these tourist homes here. I just thought they were for vacationers, which we don't get that many of anyway. Of course—It all makes sense, and Pam would keep her mouth shut about it if anybody would. She's never been one to open her mouth much on any subject."

Anyone could hear a pin drop during the short intervals my mother listened. My foot was numb from staying under my bottom for so long, I was so afraid to change my position and remind her of me.

"So they're here because of him," she said. "Why that poor little girl, and I don't think she's popular with the other girls at all."

Pins and needles in my foot and leg became unbearable. I had to stand. The book I was reading clunked to the floor.

My mother said, "I can't talk now. Little pitchers have big ears, if you know what I mean."

When she hung up, I said, "Who's he?"

"I wasn't talking to a he."

"Who did you mean when you said they're here because of *him*?"

"No one," she said. "I didn't say anything like that."

"That's an untruth," I said, which was what my grandmother always called a lie—"an untruth."

The subject was dropped.

Somewhere in our small town the subject hadn't been dropped, and the next day in school it was out in the open.

Even I drew in my breath when Marilyn Monstarr confronted you. We called her Marilyn Monster, for she was hands down the bully's bully, the meanest mouth in town, and famous for saying if you squeezed acned Carrie Speck, pus would come out.

She was saving her goodies for just before first class in the morning, while everyone was putting stuff in their lockers.

"Millicent?" she said to you in a big bully voice. "How do you like our pride and joy?"

You looked up at her while you were stooping down for books from your locker floor. You mumbled something, probably "What?"

"Our pride and joy," Marilyn Monster continued. Others were beginning to pay attention. "Our prison."

You seemed to flinch and go whiter in the face than you already were, but you managed to get out "I don't know" and shrug.

"Oh, don't you? I thought you'd know. Don't you visit your father there?"

I don't know what you did then. Finally, I was so ashamed I turned away.

Your secret was out. You and your mother had come to stay in our small town while your father served his sentence in the state prison. You in your little hat and gloves and shiny shoes, dressed so neatly and carefully, with your manicured nails, turning in the best compositions with the best penmanship and the straightest margins, were trying so hard to look and be like anything but a convict's daughter.

You made us think. I doubt that any one of us had ever thought about the relatives of the prisoners in our town before you came, though they had probably always been among us . . . staying in our many tourist homes.

You weren't with us very long. Even after your secret was out, you were never a part of us. We let up on you, but we never let you in.

After a while you went away—I don't know where or when.

But it was just as well, Millicent, because you never had a chance.

The prison in my small town had a big effect on me when I was growing up, but I was mostly caught up in the idea of a possible prison riot, or a prisoner escaping

I mention the prison in my book *Little Little*, set in the fictitious Cayuta, New York, and describe some of the feelings kids had about the prisoners as they'd come and go.

I've never forgotten Millicent, and while I never wrote about her directly, there was a lot of her in the character Opal Ringer, the have-not who thought she'd have made a real good have, in *What I Really Think of You*.

I think the experience with Millicent started me focusing in a little on the underdog. I think I felt my first real shame at how I'd treated someone, and I know that I thought of Millicent again and again as I grew up, and wished I'd never let her go without at least saying I was sorry.

In some of my books the parents wisely say the things I suppose I wished my own parents had said to me. In those books, the fictional parents try to point out that prejudice of any kind is wrong, that winning and losing in life isn't everything. But my own parents were as much the victims of their parents' prejudice as I was, and no one in my family got any extra points for being open-minded, tolerant, or particularly understanding.

Long before I ever wrote books for young adults, I wrote suspense and murder novels. I was friends with the writer Louise Fitzhugh, who longed to write murder and suspense novels. She thought I ought to write for young adults as she did. We used to laugh about it, and wonder if we traded typewriters we could perhaps each do the kind of books the other was doing.

We used to swap stories and discuss ideas, and when she wrote her first book for young people, called *Harriet the Spy*, I said, "Hey, wait a minute! That's my story! I told you I was Marijane the Spy, and you stole that idea from me!" Louise said all kids are spies when they're little. She was and I was . . . and she just beat me to the punch and told the story first.

"You'd better get going on a YA book before I beat you to the punch again," she said.

I think she's definitely one of the reasons I got going.

Four:
1, 2, 3, 4, 5, 6, 7, 8, 9,
10, 11, 12, 100!

Marijane [my father wrote in his journal] *is thirteen, and beginning to take life seriously, when she is not being the cutup of her class. Life is clothes and boys, doesn't care for anything else, writes stories, tried knitting but doesn't like it. Starts on a new budget, as follows:*

Movies, etc.	*$ 4.50*
Xmas savings	*3.00*
General savings	*2.50*
Clothes	*10.00*
	$20.00 per month

I advance 1st month and prepare ledger and budget envelopes for her.

Twelve was the age I was when my baby brother was born, and my older brother went off to military school.

Thirteen was the year I became a hundred.

Three things contributed to my rapid aging: the new baby in the house, the dramatic change in my older brother's personality, and my forced enrollment in Laura Bryan's ballroom dancing classes.

No new budget was going to make up for the fact that both my parents were suddenly swooning daily over Butchie, my baby brother.

No new budget was going to make me feel better about the sight of my older brother coming through the door on vacation from military school, a Riverside Military Academy cadet, caped and epauletted and sabered.

I was suddenly the nothing, sandwiched between two stars.

Locked in my room, I wrote stories about murder and suicide, tried on clothes, daydreamed about boys, and listened to records like "Blues in the Night" and "Let's Get Away from It All."

I was in a slump, and my mother's answer to this was to enroll me in Laura Bryan's school, this time for ballroom dancing. I had already suffered through toe and tap dancing, with Laura Bryan wincing while I performed grotesque tour jetés and did the buck-and-wing to any rhythm but the one the pianist was playing. Dancing was not one of my gifts.

William Shakespeare had moved away, and I was no longer interested in catching sunfish and pollywogs with a boy while deciding what to call our son when we were married.

I'd stopped writing to movie stars and cared less about planning dinner and setting the table for Ronald Reagan.

Boys were no longer thought of by me as good buddies I could hang out with and dress like, and go over and get at their houses.

Boys, I was beginning to perceive, were the ones who came over to your house to get you.

They were also the ones Ella Gwen Logan's mother said wouldn't buy the cow if they could get the milk free, and my own mother said made their reputations when they did it, while you lost yours if you did it.

Ella Gwen was not allowed to attend Miss Bryan's. When she *was* old enough to dance close with boys, her father'd told her, they wouldn't be just any boys whose families could afford the lessons (regardless of ethnic background).

I learned my first lesson in the power of boys at Laura Bryan's school.

You couldn't even get out on the floor without a boy choosing you for a partner. If a boy didn't choose you, you were a wallflower, which was a poor wretch, all dressed up, sitting by herself on the sidelines in a folding chair, pretending she was fascinated by her own hands.

Boys were never wallflowers.

Boys strolled around ignoring the silent plea in the wallflowers' eyes: *Pull-leeze ask me to dance, even though you have pimples and are short!* Boys didn't have to wait to be asked; they asked. If they weren't dancing, maybe they weren't in the mood. Maybe they were looking over prospective partners. Maybe they would be dancing in a second, by merely walking up to another boy who was dancing, tapping him on the shoulder, and taking the girl off.

Everyone at Laura Bryan's knew that the Paul Jones (a dance that began after you marched around to music, and danced with whomever you were in front of when the music stopped) was just a way of making boys dance with girls they'd never pick.

"She only gets to dance when a Paul Jones is played" was one way of describing a wallflower.

At age thirteen, I am sent off to the front lines, untrained and unprepared for battle.

On one side of the ballroom the boys are in a line.

Across from them, on the other side of the ballroom, the girls are in a line.

The music begins, Freddy Martin's record, "Why Don't We Do This More Often?" (I play the flip side of this record over and over, up in my room—Tschaikowsky's Piano Concerto in B Flat, better known as "Tonight We Love.")

Along with the music, the stampede begins.

Boys in dark suits, white shirts, and striped ties skid across the highly polished floor to the girls, all waiting expectantly to be chosen, in dresses (skirts and sweaters are not allowed), pumps, and hose.

A good sixty percent of the boys aim for Gloria Gilman, sliding to a halt in front of her, a tangled worms' nest of panting suitors after Gee Gee, as they always are: in school, at the skating rink, summers on the lake, in Murray's after school.

Gee Gee is that year's The One, a dark-eyed, dark-haired

Sweater Girl, with a figure no other girl at Laura Bryan's achieves without falsies stuffed down her bra.

Larry Leary gets there first, grabs her hand, claims her.

Now the boys shuffle around, looking up and down the line for second choice.

My first day at Laura Bryan's (four P.M. to five P.M. Wednesdays) I am not a boy's second choice. While the majority fight their way through themselves to Gee Gee Gilman, Clinton Klock comes galloping across to me, tall, with foul breath, perspiring palms, and bad teeth, a ninny who goes to Holy Family High School.

His love of uniforms has compelled him to enroll in Sea Scouts now that he has outgrown Boy Scouts, where he rose to the rank of Eagle Scout. One reason he is considered a ninny is that he wears his Sea Scout uniform for every special occasion.

That first day at Laura Bryan's (and thereafter) he is dressed in it. He looks like a sailor, but not being a *real* sailor, he is the butt of jokes, The Fool who is too foolish to have any notion he's one.

What he sees in me is a mystery, since he is too tall to talk to, and not encouraged by me to bend down for conversation because of his green breath. Whatever it is about me he likes remains unspoken, but at every opportunity he seeks me out, and because of him I am spared a seat on Wallflowers' Row.

"Better than nothing," my mother tells me on the way home. "Why didn't he ask you to go to Miss Margaret's with him after?"

That is the custom: Girls are asked by boys to go to Miss Margaret's for an ice-cream soda after ballroom class. Wallflowers and boys without the money for two ice cream sodas wander off to Murray's in a gang, or go home with their mothers.

"What was I going to do with you?" I answer.

"Did he ask you?"

"I wouldn't go to Miss Margaret's with him for anything! With *him* . . . pretending to be a *sailor*?" I lie . . . I would go to Miss Margaret's with someone dressed up in a monkey suit, never mind a sailor suit—just to be part of the crowd.

"Did he ask you?"

"YES, HE ASKED ME!"—another lie.

"Why are you shouting?"

"Why are you so anxious to have that ninny ask me to go for a soda?"

My mother decides not to come to Miss Bryan's to fetch me after class, in order to give me the opportunity to be invited to Miss Margaret's.

Clinton Klock's interest in me is limited to Wednesday afternoons from four P.M. to five P.M. . . . period.

As I come through the door, after the bus ride home from Laura Bryan's school, my mother is waiting. "Did you dance with Clinton Klock?"

"Yes"—yawning to affect an air of nonchalance.

"Did he ask you to go to Miss Margaret's?"

"I wouldn't go to Miss Margaret's with him for anything! With *him* . . . pretending to be a *sailor*?"

On and on, Wednesday after Wednesday, my mother ultimately delivering long lectures on the philosophy of "better than nothing" while I go up to my room, lock the door, and try to fathom the reason Seaman Klock *doesn't* ever ask me to Miss Margaret's. I am beginning to wrestle with the humiliating possibility he doesn't want to be seen in public with me . . . the ninny of the dancing class!

Easter is coming.

Normally, Easter is a favorite time of year. Easter means an extra thirty-five dollars for new clothes.

Normally, a great deal of attention is directed at me, every year at Easter. Often it involves a trip to Syracuse: to Flah's and Addises' and Dey Brothers, in search of the perfect Easter outfit for me.

This Easter is different.

My mother is busy getting Cadet Lieutenant Colonel Meaker's room ready for his arrival from military school. She is fussing over an Easter basket for the baby brother, with cookies baked in the shape of bunnies, though he is not old enough to even know what a bunny is. She is buying jelly beans and chocolate eggs and green paper hay to doll up his basket, and there is also the little outfit to be bought for him to wear to church. It is customary at Second Presbyterian Church to show up on Easter Sunday with the whole family.

I go by myself to a local store, where I buy a powder-blue 100%-virgin-wool Claire McCardell suit for $25 . . . a powder-blue hat for $3.95 . . . and patent-leather pumps for $6.75. . . .

Easter morning is awful.

The fuss at church and later at Easter dinner, at my grandparents', is over "the boys" (the sons), the new little darling one and the suddenly newly grown-up, handsome cadet.

During Easter vacation my older brother is not even any longer my blood enemy, punching me and teasing me and nyah-nyahing at me from his room. He is courteous and remote, and he is busy calling up a local girl for dates.

Up in my room I write a poem one afternoon when everyone is gone, nearly vomiting from smoking a Chesterfield cigarette I have found in my brother's overcoat pocket.

Christ, you didn't die for me,

I compose and cough,

I am already dead!

After Easter vacation, one Wednesday at Laura Bryan's, *I* say to Clinton Klock, "Why don't we go to Miss Margaret's for sodas after?"

"I'm saving all my money for a boat," he tells me.

"Dutch treat," I suggest.

"I'm saving every cent," he persists.

"I'll treat," I announce.

I have no way of knowing he will one day be the fabulous Tick Tock Klock, leading Holy Family High to victory in all basketball games, his halitosis gone, his name on every Catholic girl's lips, his bad teeth forgotten . . . his Sea Scout uniform packed away in his attic.

I have him in his formative years, and I sit with him ultimately in Miss Margaret's over black-and-white sodas, raising my eyes to the ceiling, unfairly, when he isn't looking, for the benefit of my girl friends, as if to signal: *I have died and gone to hell!*

Other girls with boys not up to snuff go for the laughs, too. This is the only advantage girls have over boys: Everyone knows that when you're in Miss Margaret's, the *boys* did the inviting . . . so the boys can't claim *they're* stuck with duds.

No one present has any way of knowing *I* am treating the very one I am pretending is Life's Biggest Embarrassment to me.

From there on it is all downhill.

"Did you hear the one about the couple on their wedding night?" Clinton's opener as we sit waiting for our sodas at the round table with wrought-iron legs. (I have already slipped him the money taken from my general savings envelope, to pay the check.)

I tell him I haven't heard it, knowing I probably have. I have heard more jokes about wedding nights than Clinton has brown teeth in his mouth. But I am following some of my father's advice, to pretend that I've never heard any joke a boy is about to tell. The part of the advice I won't follow is not to laugh at the joke if it is dirty. Boys don't know any other kind of joke. Girls don't either, and tell even more than boys do, but girls usually tell them only to other girls, behind their hands.

"Well, this couple on their wedding night had a room next to the elevator"—ha ha to himself as he tries to continue without breaking up altogether. "The next day the hotel manager says, 'Did you enjoy your honeymoon night here?' Well, this guy answers—he's thinking about the elevator, see—he answers, 'It was just up and down, up and down, all night long!' "

Clinton slaps the table with his hand and howls and says, "Get it? Get it? Up and down. And it's his wedding night!"

"Hilarious," I say, choking out a guffaw.

"Isn't it hilarious? The hotel manager doesn't know he means the elevator."

"I got it, I got it," I say.

"He thinks he means—"

"Natch," I put in, before he gets any more graphic. "*Naturellement.*"

"Did you hear the one about—"

On and on.

For this display of great wit I have sacrificed myself to my mother's dream of having her daughter invited to Miss Margaret's with Better Than Nothing.

With this I am putting up, to be part of the crowd who don't herd off to Murray's after dancing school, or straight home via mothers and buses.

When we leave Miss Margaret's, there is Clinton's mother out front in the family's green DeSoto. She offers to drive me home, and I'm squeezed into the front seat between them, while Mrs. Klock rattles on about the Nazi blitz raids over London.

As I come through the front door this time, I am ready and waiting for the big question: *Did he ask you to go to Miss Margaret's?*

My mother takes off in another direction, beginning, "Poor Eleanor Klock, Marijane! And I'm so embarrassed."

"What's the matter with Mrs. Klock?" I ask.

"Whatever got into you to tell Clinton *you'd* buy *him* a soda! When he called his mother to tell her why he'd be late getting home, she felt so ashamed, she got dressed and got out the car, to give you a ride home! She said Clinton has money of his own, but he's saving for a boat, and she felt just awful!"

I myself feel like throwing up.

"Girls don't ask boys to go to Miss Margaret's!" my mother says.

I head up the stairs for my room.

"You have too much money to throw around!" she calls after me. "Your allowance is way too high!"

Then the kicker. "If you've got so much spare money, why don't you buy your baby brother a toy? You never think of him!"

———————

That summer, wadded up in my brother's wastebasket, I find the beginnings of a series of unfinished notes to Eloise Antonio, a girl he is "seeing."

We have seen very little of him all summer, but his presence is felt: in dents in my father's car; on nights when he's not home *yet*; during daytime forays into his room (while he's at work in my father's factory) as my mother searches for signs he's smoking, drinking, and all the other ings he's not supposed to be inging.

These notes I straighten out on my desk top and examine:

My dearest Eloise, I think all the zombies I drank
made me forget—

My darling Eloise, I know you're not that kind of girl. All the zombies—

My sweetest Elly, I love and respect you though you'd never know it after all those zombies. I—

I decide a good thing to do with these incomplete messages is to wait until he comes home for dinner, and then sing them out like songs, one after the other, moments before everyone sits down at the table.

No longer courteous and remote, he makes a flying tackle at me when I'm halfway through my performance, and we land on the floor in a kicking, socking, screaming tangle.

My father grabs us both by our collars and shakes us to our feet.

I wait for him to give it to my brother.

Not only has my brother knocked me down, but what about the contents of those notes I put to music?

"Don't you *ever* go through your brother's wastebasket again!" says my hero.

This is my hero?

"What?" I can't be-*lieve* it.

"Your brother has a right to his privacy!"

"What about what he's doing with Elo—"

"That's not your business!"

"Ant, ant, ant, wahhhhhhhhhhh!" from the other brother, upset by all the noise.

"Now see what you've done!"—my mother, rushing to pick him up from his high chair in the dining room.

"Go to your room without supper!" my father commands,

which is better, anyway, than going down to the cellar during supper.

My last memory of my thirteenth-going-on-one-hundred-and-first year was a Sunday afternoon in December.

My brother was back in military school, and "the other one" (my favorite designation for him) had been bundled up in his little blue snowsuit that matched his eyes, and taken off for a sleigh ride by my father.

Before "the other one" had come into being, on cold winter afternoons I often went skating with my father, down at the same pond in Hoopes Park where I'd once fished with William Shakespeare.

I was alone in my room, brooding, trying to get interested in a new book called *What Makes Sammy Run?* about Hollywood. An Ella Gwen Logan recommendation.

Enter my mother.

"One thing that's wrong with you," she began (in the Andy Hardy movies, did kindly old Judge Hardy ever begin his heart-to-heart talks with his son on such a negative note?), "is that you're determined to be the funny girl."

She sat down on my bed, where I was stretched out, and I flinched from the physical contact we would have had if I hadn't moved my leg fast.

"Daisy Porter tells me you're the school clown."

"She teaches French," I said, "and she never leaves her room, so she doesn't know anything that goes on in the rest of the school. And everyone knows the reason she never leaves her room, too!"

"I'm not talking about Daisy Porter. I'm talking about you."

"The reason she never leaves her room is she has corns and it's hard for her to even walk, she has so many. She buys corn pads by the billions from Daw's Drugs, and also millions and millions of bottles of bunion medicine. Jimmy Keene works there and he's told us all, so that's why she never even gets up from her desk between classes."

"I'm talking about *you*. I'm telling you this for your own good. Boys don't like girls who cut up."

"I'm not living my life for what boys like."

"They don't like girls who crack jokes all the time and are bent on being comedians."

"Who cares? Who cares? Who cares?"

"You're going to care, pull-lenty, when all the other girls get boyfriends and you don't. You'll be the comedian, hah? There isn't a female comedian alive who's happy," said my mother. "Oh, they get up onstage and get laughs and make fools out of themselves, let their faces and bodies get into all sorts of ungraceful positions, but when the curtain comes down, it's another story."

"How do *you* know?"

"Everyone knows that! Do you think Martha Raye is a happy woman?"

"I don't think about Martha Raye."

"Or Fanny Brice?"

"I don't think about her, either. I don't care about those old movie stars and if they're happy."

"Well, you better start thinking about them, and they're not *stars*, they're comedians," my mother said. "You'd better start thinking about all the other Hollywood types who let their femininity go down the drain to get a few laughs! They turn into very unhappy women. Do you think Betty Hutton's happy?"

On and on, until she was finally interrupted by the telephone.

She went to answer it, and I sat up on my bed with my knuckles in my mouth, planning a possible revenge on Miss Porter. How about scotch-taping an advertisement for a corn remedy to her blackboard? . . . No, this deserved something worse. Some of those in my French class had already taped up an advertisement about bad breath; Daisy Porter was known for the worst breath in Fulton School, only because Clinton Klock was at Holy Family High.

I'd had nothing to do with the toothpaste ad put up on her blackboard.

TOO BAD FOR DAVY,
HE HAS THE DOUBLE O.

The "double O" was Listerine jargon for offensive breath/offensive teeth.

DAVY had been changed to DAISY, and "he" had been changed to "she."

I knew Miss Porter thought I was in on that one, and called my mother to complain about me in general.

I was dreaming up something to get even, something like Alka-Seltzer tablets dropped into the inkwells on everyone's desk, just as the class was leaving the room, so the ink would rise up and spill over like dozens of tiny erupting volcanoes.

My mother was back in my room.

I noticed she'd come in wringing her hands.

"What's the matter now?" I said.

I was waiting to hear Miss St. Amour had followed with a phone call after Miss Porter's, or Miss James had, or Miss Hallohan, or Miss Fish, or Mr. Murphy . . . there wasn't anyone in the whole school I trusted except my English teacher, who said I was a good writer.

"What did I do now?" I said.

"It's really bad news," she said. "We've been bombed in someplace called Pearl Harbor."

"I never even heard of it," I said.

"I haven't, either, but the Japanese bombed us there, and I think we're at war. That's what Grandma Meaker just said."

Across the street our neighbors, the Hunters, were just hearing the news that one of the battleships sunk at Pearl Harbor was the *Oklahoma*.

Their only son, Hooton, was aboard.

No longer would The War be talked about in fragmented ways by people like Clinton Klock's mother, making conversation while she took her son's "friend" home . . . "Oh, they're blitzing poor London," she'd said . . . and as the new year began, Clinton, I, all us kids were learning how to act during air raid drills, finding out what blackouts were, and saying good-bye to boys a few years ahead of us in school.

"War," I remember my mother repeating, sitting on my bed while we waited for my radio to warm up, so we could hear the news. "War. It's come." Then she let out a long sigh and said what she so often said in times of crisis.

"Oh, shoot!" clapping her hand across her mouth when she realized what had come out of it.

In my books for young adults, I updated everything that happened to me in my teens, to make my stories more contemporary, probably not trusting the idea I could interest today's kids in yesterday's happenings.

I knew I could interest today's kids in yesterday's kids, because they're the same kids. I probably wouldn't set a novel in 1941, but I wouldn't hesitate to write about a kid from the forties, and make him or her a kid in the eighties.

What's going on in the world is secondary to what's going on in high school, for in those vulnerable teen years high school *is* the world. There, a kid begins to get the first real feelings of being on his/her own; there, the idea of winning and losing starts taking shape, of being in or out, part of the crowd, or an outsider. . . . There, adults other than parents become role models or enemies or objects of ridicule. . . . And with all that going on, there are changes going on at home, as kids begin to see things they hadn't noticed before: the way their parents get along, or don't, the way their own brothers and sisters are coping.

There is a lot of the real "yesterday me" in *Dinky Hocker Shoots Smack!*, and in *The Son of Someone Famous*.

I think that whenever you find a little smart-mouth, tomboy kid in any of my books, you have found me from long ago, but

Dinky Hocker and Brenda Belle Blossom, in particular, were so me I hardly had to think up their lines.

I didn't have much trouble thinking up their mothers' lines, either.

Whatever truce was reached between my mother and me was reached very late in life, and remains shaky. It helped a lot that I had grown up to be a writer, with published books, although never enough to make up for the fact that in her view I'd "missed the boat."

"What boat is that?" I asked her when she brought the subject up, during one of our phone conversations.

"You know very well what boat," said she. "It's the same boat my grandchildren would be on. You missed that boat."

I said that at least I hadn't become one of these unhappy female comedians.

She said, "Well, I'm not sure you're so happy being this female writer, either."

Two of my books, I discovered long after I'd written them— *The Son of Someone Famous* and *Little Little*—end with the statement "My mother's right"; but of course, my mother knew that all along, without reading it in any book I'd written.

For a while my mother took a great interest in my books for young adults, more than she had in my adult suspense books, where in two instances a mother is murdered. I think she stopped reading Kerr after *Is That You, Miss Blue?* The first-person narrator is a young girl who went to a boarding school similar to the one I went to, and came from a small town in upstate New York, as I did. Her mother ran off with a man years younger than herself while the heroine was a teenager. . . . I think that was the last book of mine my mother read.

So far my brothers haven't appeared in any of my books, and

perhaps this is my way of crossing them out, as I sometimes wanted to when I was in my early teens and they were The Sons. . . . But I hope it is just because I haven't gotten around to them yet.

The real Tick Tock Klock became a real sailor and was killed in World War II.

Five:
There's Not a Man
in This Damn Nunnery!

The song was taught to me on the train to Stuart Hall, in Staunton, Virginia.

Jan Fox taught it to me.

She was an "old girl" and I was a "new girl," but we were both northerners, the only ones on the train.

We are the girls from Stuart Hall, you see,
There's not a man in this damn nunnery,
And every night at eight they lock the door,
I don't know why the hell I ever came before,
And when at Christmastime I'm homeward bound,
I'm going to turn the damn town upside down,

I'm going to drink and smoke and neck and pet,
Yes, by heck! The hell with Stuart Hall!

Our chaperone for the trip was a faculty member named Miss Stone, who preferred the smoker to our car, though she checked on us from time to time.

We'd all met at the Information booth in Grand Central Station, where Miss Stone had stood with a Stuart Hall catalogue under her arm so I could identify her.

"She's having a nervous breakdown," Jan told me when the train started and Miss Stone went off where she could smoke.

"How do you know?"

"She thinks she was reincarnated from Ludwig van Beethoven. If you take music from her, you'll hear all about it," said Jan Fox, and then she said, "Oh, damnation, I've run my stocking!"

Then she went on to say, "All the teachers are crazy. There's something wrong with every one of them. You'll see."

It did not even take me the time it took the train to reach Washington, D.C., to know that Jan Fox was the most sophisticated person I had ever met in my entire life.

Would they all be like that at Stuart Hall?

Jan Fox was still tanned from the summer sun, tall with long red hair that spilled to her shoulders, blue eyed and long legged, a beauty who said, "Damnation!" and carried a package of Old Gold cigarettes in her purse.

"You can't smoke at Stuart Hall, can you?" I asked her.

"You're not supposed to. You can get expelled for it. Cigarettes are contraband, along with liquor and candy. But sometimes I go crazy if I don't have a drag, so I sneak a puff in my closet."

She was everything I wasn't. I had some kind of navy-blue beanie type hat on my head; she had on a white hat with a long green feather. My thin hair, which I rolled up on curlers every night, had wilted in the humidity and hung like wet string. I'd been called a "dishwater blonde" by my mother.

Jan Fox's red hair looked good straight, and was supposed to be straight. It was thick and wavy.

I had on some very tailored navy-blue suit with a white blouse, white gloves, and blue-and-white spectator pumps.

She had on a white skirt, and a green-and-white-checked jacket, with a white cashmere sweater. She wore white heels, with sling backs and open toes.

I knew the instant I met her that I didn't have the right clothes for boarding school.

As we traveled along toward Virginia, I realized I didn't have the right face, right body, right personality, right background, or anything right for boarding school.

Back at the beginning of that summer, when I was choosing boarding schools from the back of *Good Housekeeping* magazine, and sending away for their catalogues, I'd thought the only thing wrong with my life was where I was living it. All I needed, I told myself, was to fly the coop, get out from under, get away to a better life without brothers around and where the rules were the same for everyone. (I was the only girl I knew, after Ella Gwen Logan eloped, who still couldn't go in cars with boys.)

In the presence of Jan Fox, I began to see that I'd gone from the frying pan to the fire.

After she taught me the words to the song about there not being a man in the damn nunnery, she told me more about Stuart Hall.

She told me there were only four reasons anyone got sent there:

1. You were intelligent and pitiful, a scholarship student.

2. Your parents were social climbers, and wanted you in a fancy school.

3. You were in the way at home.

4. You were out of the ordinary, like a dwarf.

"Which one are you?" she asked me. "I'm a two."

"I'm not any of them," I said. "I'm a five."

"What's a five?"

· "A five is someone who's not any of those four."

"Why were you sent away then?" she asked.

"I wanted to go away," I said, "because I'm tired of my brothers, and my father's the strictest man in town, and my mother is afraid I'm going to grow up to be an unhappy female comedian. They weren't even going to let me go away, until I helped my best friend elope. Then I guess they decided they couldn't control me."

"That makes you a three," Jan Fox said. "If they can't control you, you're just in the way."

I decided to change the subject.

"Where do your parents social climb?" I said.

"Wherever they are. They're divorced. He social climbs all over the world because he's this big corporate lawyer, and she socializes in Palm Beach, Palm Springs . . . places like that. We're not small-town people."

Then she said, "I'm going to teach you the signal for Miss Stone. We all give it at school when she comes on the scene. It's like the four notes in the V for Victory—listen." She went "Da, da, da, daaaaa."

She said, "It's from Beethoven's Fifth, since she thinks she was him once. Have you got it?"

"I've heard it before," I said.

"Well, give it if you see her coming," she said. "I'm going to light up. I'll go crazy if I don't have a few drags."

She wasn't the only one lighting up in that car. It was jammed with servicemen, some standing in the aisles and many sneaking smokes. But my heart pounded while she leaned down for some puffs on her Old Gold, and I watched anxiously with the four notes from Beethoven's Fifth ready, sure I was going to be expelled from boarding school before I even arrived.

But I took a drag anyway, when she offered it, eager to impress her.

Then she put out the cigarette and kicked it away from the floor in front of us.

"Oh gawd, we needed that!" she said.

"We sure did," I managed to get out, dizzy from the little taste of nicotine, my stomach turning over in shock.

"Now I'll tell you what to expect tonight," she said. "You'll be over in Robertson House with the other juniors, but some seniors will be by later for the test."

"A test on the first night?"

"The school isn't giving it," she said. "The seniors are, and only to the new juniors."

"What's it a test on?" I asked.

"Sex. They want to know how much experience you've had. Just make it up!"

Then she said, "Damnation! Here comes Miss Stone! I need a Lifesaver for my breath, or she'll know I've smoked a weed!"

She began to root around in her purse for one.

My roommate was named Kay Walters, and she was a preacher's kid—a P.K. from Pennsylvania.

She had been there for a day, but in the space of a few hours I told her all that Jan had told me, more than she'd have probably learned in a month.

When a knock came on our door that night, and a voice from the hall said the Senior Committee wanted to come in, I said, "Damnation! They've come to give us the test!"

"What test?"

"The sex test," I said. "Don't you even know about that?"

Then I explained that they were going to ask us how much experience we had.

"Don't let them in," she said. "I haven't had any!"

"Just make it up," I said. "I haven't had a lot, but more than most small-town people," I lied.

We let the seniors in, and they passed out mimeographed sheets. You were to check the box if the answer was "yes" to such questions as:

Did you ever go all the way?
Half the way?
A quarter of the way?
Have you let a boy unbutton your blouse?
Have you ever been in the backseat of a car with a boy?

There were questions on that sheet I didn't even know the meaning of, and descriptions of things I'd never even thought of, but I rapidly checked all the boxes and handed back my sheet.

"Gawd!" I exclaimed. "I'll go crazy if I don't have a weed!"

One of the seniors was eyeing me scornfully.

Another was looking over my test. Then Kay's.

Kay said meekly, "I'm a preacher's kid." The three seniors conferred for a while in a corner of the room.

"I didn't check anything," Kay whispered to me.

"I told you to make it up," I said.

"I didn't even know what half the things meant!" she said.

"Where have *you* been?" I said.

The senior who'd eyed me scornfully was turning around. I'd hoped my test would change her expression, maybe to awe; at least to one of admiration.

But her eyes were dark and mean and narrow.

"Since you've had such a vast sexual background," she said to me, "all the seniors will come by tomorrow before dinner, for a sex education lecture from you."

Another senior said, "You'll lecture for ten minutes on questions eleven, twelve, and thirteen. Then you'll take questions from the audience for another five minutes. . . . Be ready at five-thirty tomorrow afternoon."

The third senior touched Kay's shoulder. "Welcome to Stuart Hall," she said. "You'll do just fine here."

After they'd left, I grabbed the sheet and looked at eleven, twelve, and thirteen.

"Oh, damnation!" I groaned. "Those three are the hard ones. I mean, I don't know that much about those three."

"I think that test was a trap," Kay said. "I think we weren't supposed to know that much about any of it."

"I think you're right," I said.

"What are you going to do?" she said.

"I'm not going to be here tomorrow," I said. "Not at five-thirty."

"They'll get you," she said. "If you're not here, they'll get you some way."

"They won't get me," I said.

But they would; they did.

From that day forward, for as long as I was in Robertson House, I was at war with certain seniors, and nearly all the faculty.

I had very definitely gotten myself started on the wrong foot.

The headmistress of Stuart Hall was a formidable woman who, angered, left notes in your mailbox saying:

See me at once! APH!

Because of her initials, we called her Ape.

I regularly found notes from Ape in my mailbox, almost more often than I found mail from home there, though my father wrote faithfully at least once a week.

Jan Fox had a single room in Main Building, and I almost never saw her.

The other girls at Stuart Hall were not at all like Jan Fox.

She was in a class by herself, and in one of the rare single rooms by herself, at her family's request.

She was a loner, caught up in a love affair with a cadet from Staunton Military Academy whose rank was much higher than my own brother's, and who was called H.P.

She seemed to have forgotten all about any intimacy we'd shared on the train, and looked through me when we passed in the halls.

I knew the war I was waging with the other seniors, and the faculty, was my own personal war—there'd be no help from Jan Fox.

But the juniors from Robertson gave me some moral support for my battles, eager for any excitement to break the monotonous routine in a school that didn't allow radios, boys on campus (except for rare dances), lights on after ten at night, or weekends away from school.

We did not even get Saturdays off, since the streets of Staunton were filled with SMA cadets on Saturdays. We got Mondays off, instead, and signed up for shopping or movies in small groups always led by a faculty member.

After a while I was not even allowed Mondays in town, since I always seemed to be in trouble.

The whole school operated by "the bell," which was rung by pulling an enormous rope in Main Building. All classes, meals, study hours—everything was coordinated by this bell, which I sawed in half with a carving knife, stolen from the kitchen, my second week there.

Seniors I was at war with found they could not work up a lather on their personal bars of soap, since I'd sneaked in and covered each one with clear nail polish.

Inkwells in classrooms overflowed, as I dropped in Alka-Seltzer tablets.

I organized a small atheist club, and got the members to always sing hymns in chapel and church backward.

Nation and man every to once,

my followers sang to 433 in our *Common Prayer/Hymnal* book,

Decide to moment the comes. . . .

Even Kay, the P.K., belonged to our club for a while.

I wrote Earl Browder, president of the Communist Party, explaining that I was in a preparatory school in the south, and a great many of the girls were interested in joining the party. I received a letter back directing me to an organization in Richmond, Virginia. I wrote them and joined their group, paying $1.50 membership fee, and $7.50 in subscriptions for party newspapers and educational information.

The Daily Worker, the official Communist newspaper, was sent to my box regularly, and I gleaned enough information to make posters saying such things as:

ABANDON THE UNFAIR POLL TAX!

tacking them up on the school bulletin boards. . . . This did not go over well in a southern school in the forties. Blacks, known then as Negroes, were prevented from voting in many southern states, because they could not afford to pay a poll tax.

Near Christmas Ape went ape, grabbing me one morning in assembly after the singing of "We Walk by Faith" ("Sight by not and faith by walk we") and pulling me along to her office.

"After Christmas vacation, you're going to have a new room," she said. "You'll no longer be in Robertson House. You're a disruptive influence."

"Where will I be?"

"Where will I be, Mrs. Hodges, please?" she corrected me.

"Where will I be, Mrs. Hodges, please?"

"You will be in Main Building on Middle Music Hall."

"Middle Music Hall only has little rooms with pianos in them."

"We are taking out a piano and putting in a bed, bureau, desk, and chair."

I said nothing; there was nothing to be said.

Middle Music Hall was surrounded by halls named after Charles Dickens' novels . . . halls like Little Dorrit, Nicholas Nickleby, and David Copperfield. (I was to rename Middle Music "Hard Times.")

As I was leaving her office, she said, "You are to write to

that newspaper and have your subscription stopped immediately!"

"Yes, Mrs. Hodges."

"And you are to tell them not to send any other tawdry literature to this address!"

Marijane came home December 16, a pretty and vivacious young lady [wrote my father in his journal], *but her semiannual report received yesterday was a new low, and Mrs. Hodges wrote that unless she improves, grades and particularly conduct, she will not be invited back next year. I leave a letter on Marijane's desk telling her if she is not asked back, she can't continue school, but will have to go to work and live at home. No late nights, no use of cars, no dates. Send copy of letter to Mrs. Hodges.*

On the train going back to school, after Christmas vacation, I encountered Jan Fox again, and the reincarnation of Ludwig van Beethoven.

Jan was wearing a mink cape over a bright-red wool suit, with a mink hat.

Very few of us at school had fur coats, and I had never seen anyone from school in mink before.

I drew my cloth coat around me, and didn't attempt conversation as the three of us boarded the train.

Miss Stone hurried ahead to the smoking car, and I was about to sit next to a soldier when Jan Fox grabbed my hand and said, "There's a seat for two over there. You have to sit with me," she said. "You're my lookout."

"You never pay any attention to me in school," I complained.

"I hate that Robertson House clique," she said. "All cliques bore me to death."

"Well, I'm not part of a clique anymore," I said, and I told her about being moved to Middle Music.

"How could Ape put you there?" she said. "You have to be deaf to live there! They practice piano, violin, trumpet—whatever instrument anyone plays, they play there!"

"I'll get cotton for my ears," I said. I didn't want anyone in a mink coat starting to pity me.

"Wait, it gets worse!" she said. "Do you know who they put on Middle Music? Number fours! Always! Dwarfs, pinheads—you name it! It's where they put out-of-the-ordinarys!"

"It's just a trial period," I lied. "I might even be moved to a single somewhere else next month."

"A single somewhere else? They're all taken. There're only three, and I have one. Pauline Paul has one because of her asthma, and Caroline Day has the third. You have to arrange a year in advance for one."

I changed the subject of Middle Music Hall.

"How come you have one?"

"Because everyone my age is childish," she said. "I'm old for my age. I'd be bored to death rooming with anyone my age."

"I don't like roommates, either," I lied. I'd spent most of Christmas vacation already missing Kay, even though she swore to me we'd still be good friends.

"I spent my whole vacation going to nightclubs with H.P. in New York," she said. "I had so many martinis they were coming out of my ears."

"I prefer zombies," I said. I'd never even seen one, only the word, written in my brother's unfinished notes to Eloise Antonio.

"Zombies are for kids," she said. "Adults drink martinis, Manhattans, whiskey sours—real cocktails, not fruit punch with a thimble of booze."

"I, myself, like a pink lady now and then," I said. The few times my mother and her friends went to the country club for lunch, they all ordered pink ladies.

"That's a hick drink," Jan Fox said. "Only kids and hicks drink that."

"I don't come from a drinking family." I gave up the contest. "We're all Presbyterians."

She accepted my surrender with enthusiasm, pushed her mink cape off her shoulders, and gave me a big smile. "I'll teach you what's chic," she said. "Now that you're out of Robertson House and over in Main, I'll take you under my wing."

"I'm going to be a writer," I said. "That's my ambition."

"Do you know what mine is?"

"What's yours?"

"To have a drag on a cigarette. I'll go crazy if I don't have one right this deadly second!"

"I'll watch for Miss Stone," I said.

I was beginning to get the knack of having a friendship with Jan Fox.

That night, alone in my room (more like a cell—no sink, just a bed, bureau, desk, and chair), I was talking myself into accepting my fate, since the alternative was living at home, working in some factory like Columbian Rope, being driven around by my parents, and not being allowed to date.

The lights-out bell rang, and I settled down in the dark, almost asleep, when I heard a wailing unlike any I had ever heard, not human, it couldn't be. A ghost? I didn't know. I froze. I listened. I heard it again and again.

If I'd been able to think clearly, I would have realized one thing about myself I'd never known before that moment: Whatever I would die of in this life, it would not be fright. If fright could have done it, I would have been dead already.

But I was as good as dead. Because when my door opened slowly, I was paralyzed.

"Dear? Are you awake?" a voice called out.

It was Miss Woodland's voice I heard as I lay there paralyzed. Then the overhead light in my small room was snapped on.

I was no longer powerless; I sat up in bed with my heart pounding, rubbing my eyes against the light.

Miss Woodland was the faculty chum for David Copperfield Hall, around the corner from Middle Music.

Because of her last name we called her "Timber." She taught science, but was most known for the enormous cross she always wore around her neck, and her religious fanaticism.

She had on an old blue wool bathrobe, which matched her intense blue eyes, covering a long pink nightie. Her gray hair, usually back in a bun, was loose, and fell down past her shoulders.

"I'm sorry, dear," she said, "but your new hallmate has arrived, and I thought it would be nice if you became acquainted before morning."

"What was that terrible wailing in the hall just a second ago?" I asked.

"There's something you should know about your new hallmate."

"Is she a ghost? Why is she arriving in the middle of the school year?"

"Dear, Agnes is a very lovely young lady whose family has decided she would be helped here. You see, she's deaf. She doesn't hear at all."

Then Timber stepped back and gave my door a tiny push with her bedroom slipper, and there stood this girl.

"This is Agnes Thatcher, dear." Miss Woodland turned her back to me and said in a very slow and precise voice, and also loudly, "Agnes, this is Marijane Meaker."

Before I tell you what Agnes Thatcher said, let me tell you what she looked like.

She was short, and very slender, with shoulder-length hair so white-gold that at first I thought it wasn't real. Her eyes were light green, and she had pale, soft-looking skin, and her wide, full lips were smiling. She looked like some enchanted angel.

She said—she wailed—"OWWWWWL!" She seemed to lunge forward at me as she made this sound, with her mouth forming a large O.

"That means hello," said Miss Woodland, noticeably rattled by the sound herself.

"Hi!" I said, speaking very loudly, too, and making an exaggerated hi with my mouth.

She said, "Lo leet you."

"Pleased to meet you. That means pleased to meet you," said Miss Woodland.

Again I worked my lips laboriously, answering, "Same here," and speaking in a loud voice.

Then Agnes said, "Gite."

I frowned when Miss Woodland failed to translate for me, and I saw Miss Woodland frowning, too.

"What?" I made my mouth say, my voice shout.

This time Agnes barked the word at me, leaning closer to my face as though she was going to spit in my eye. "GITE!"

I just sat there, looking away from her, smoothing the ribbon along my blanket's edge.

Miss Woodland said, "Well, now that you've met . . ." and her voice trailed off.

I whispered, "I don't know what she wants, or what 'gite' means."

"It's all right, dear. You're both acquainted," said Miss Woodland.

The next thing, Agnes Thatcher stamped her feet and shook her head and tried to say more forcibly the sound "gite," but it became a long, wailing, "GIIIIIIIIIIIIIIIIIIITE!"

Her eyes were narrowed and she was showing great irritation with both of us for not understanding. She was also carefully watching our lips. It would do no good for me to whisper, and I needn't have stretched my mouth all out of proportion, for she obviously was an excellent lip-reader.

I looked at her and shrugged my shoulders, smiling a little. "I just don't get it," I said.

She didn't smile back. She gave a heavy sigh and shook her head angrily.

"Well, I'm glad you're both acquainted." Miss Woodland kept harping on the notion of our acquaintance, as though the mere fact of our meeting had been the primary obstacle to overcome. She said. "I think we better say good night."

At this, Agnes Thatcher grabbed her arm, gave it a punch, put one finger up in the air, and shook her head up and down in a "yes" gesture.

Then she said again, "Gite."

Still we didn't get it.

"We have to say good night, dear," Miss Woodland said.

Agnes shook her head harder, shook her finger at Miss Woodland, and repeated, "Gite!"

"Good night," I said. "Is that it?"

She came dancing across to my bed with a big grin, and then, leaning down, she socked me in the shoulder. "Gite," she said.

I laughed, even though she hit hard and it hurt.

"Good night, Agnes."

"Gite."

"See you tomorrow."

"Lo leet you."

"Right," I said.

"Gite." She was backing out of the room with Miss Woodland following.

I gave a little two-fingered salute with my hand. "So long."

As she disappeared from view, Miss Woodland's hand still remained in my room, and I heard her shout, "Just a moment, Agnes. I'll come to tuck you in."

Her face and part of her body reappeared in my room.

"Isn't that sad, dear?" she said. "Jesus allows our afflictions to test us, but we sometimes forget 'His will be done' when we see the stricken."

"Is she next door to me?" I said. I knew she was. I could already hear her slamming things around in there, but I didn't want to go on talking with Miss Woodland in that vein, about "the stricken" and "His will be done." I didn't take to the idea of God or Jesus (if there even was One) treating whoever He felt like treating the same way a vivisectionist might treat a stray dog, testing someone's faith the way the dog might be tested for the physical side effects of a new drug.

"She's in eight, yes, dear. She's going to get along just fine. No special privileges to be granted to her, either. Her family wants her to participate in whatever the others participate in, be judged as they're judged."

I could hear hangers falling on the closet floor next door, and suitcases thumping against the walls. Since she could not hear herself, I doubted that she would be the quietest neighbor.

"I'll go to her now," said Miss Woodland. "Good night, dear."

"Gite," I said.

Gradually I made myself become oblivious to the chunking

of baggage against walls, the slamming of drawers, and the wailing interspersed with Miss Woodland's shouts. They were background noises, like the sounds of workers putting up a house next to yours, I told myself. I'd get used to it . . . I'd get used to it.

Then the noises stopped; the reflection of her light on the ivy outside my windowsill was gone.

I sank down under the covers.

About five minutes later I heard what sounded like an angry elephant charging, followed by a sound like air seeping from the tire of a huge trailer truck . . . angry elephant, air seeping, angry elephant, air seeping.

Of course. Agnes Thatcher snored.

During those years of World War II, "boyfriends" materialized in the mail as randomly and spontaneously as dandelions on a summer lawn, all of them servicemen. Old high school friends wrote from camps and bases and forts, and friends of brothers in the service wrote. Girl friends' brothers wrote, and even soldiers and sailors you met on trains en route to school wrote.

Nearly every girl in school corresponded with a boy in the service.

Nearly everyone in school had a relative in the service, too.

Yet except for the times we traveled to and from school, and spent at home on vacations, the war couldn't have seemed more far away, nor more unreal.

Nothing about the war was taught in our classes—the Civil War was, from a strangely biased southern point of view, but the "real war" went unmentioned, perhaps *because* so many of us could have been affected by the news.

Since we had no radios, we didn't even know of our victories, much less our defeats . . . and we even lost touch with the minimal hardships like rationing and shortages others were aware of at home.

Donald Dare had dropped out of my life after a short-lived attempt at corresponding. I was busy writing a boy from my hometown I hardly knew, and one I knew just about as well who'd been a friend of my brother's before he joined the Marines.

His name was Buck, and he liked to decorate the envelopes he sent his letters in with hearts severed by daggers and our initials, and other initials like the old cliché SWAK (sealed with a kiss).

But I wrote notes far more to my next-door neighbor, Agnes Thatcher, than I did to servicemen . . . and to others at school—Kay, my ex-roommate with whom I was rapidly losing touch, Jan Fox, and anyone who could be recruited into plots against the school, my atheist club, and my vendetta against the elite and privileged organization known as the E.L.A.

The latter invited a few select girls each year to become members, and the rest of us came upon them in the halls performing various pantomine routines as part of their initiation. They went about frying like eggs and flushing like toilets . . . and soon, we all knew, they would be allowed to go into a special room where only they could go to hang out . . . and they would be allowed to keep the library.

No one was supposed to ever know what E.L.A. stood for,

but I put it all together one day while I was in the library, where I always was, anyway, being a library addict.

I saw a bulletin from the Episcopal Library Association . . . and I realized the E.L.A. (we called them the Extra Lucky Asses) always had library duties, along with their special privileges.

That night, Agnes Thatcher and I scrawled across blackboards in Main Building *E.L.A. means Episcopal Library Association* . . . and we thumbtacked the same notice on a large piece of cardboard to the bulletin board in Main.

By then Agnes was my great buddy, happy to be in on all my mischief, unhappy with me only when I stole her fresh white wool socks—she seemed to have an endless supply, and when she spotted them on my feet, she followed me crying out "Dock! Dock! Dock!"—her way of saying "socks"—oblivious to my revelation that she sounded like a duck calling out.

Mrs. Hodges knew Agnes and I had become pals. We spent our Mondays together always, while others went on chaperoned jaunts to movies and soda shops in town. Agnes felt people stared at her when she opened her mouth, so she refused to go on these trips, and I as often as not was being campused for some infraction of the rules, and couldn't go.

The day after the E.L.A. exposure, Agnes was called into Mrs. Hodges' office. Ape took her pencil out (breaking the point as she wrote, Agnes told me later): *Did you and Marijane write out those E.L.A. notices?*

Agnes was a good lip-reader and didn't like questions written out for her.

She looked at Ape's message, took out her pen, and wrote back, *What?*

Later, with the threat that Ape would campus everyone until the culprits stepped forward, I confessed.

I can't remember all she promised would happen to me if I continued on my errant way, but I remember I was room campused for one month. That meant I had to stay in my room during all my free time, "and give some thought to the fact you've broken a hundred-year-old tradition by revealing what E.L.A. means."

"Yes, ma'am," I said.

Then she said, "And another thing. No more of those tawdry pieces of mail are to come to your box again!"

Tawdry was her favorite anathema.

"I haven't had any communication with the Communists since Christmas, when you told me to stop their mail!" I said.

"I don't mean the Communists this time," said she. "I mean envelopes from that serviceman who draws vulgar figures on them, and puts initials across them standing for tawdry sayings! Write to him immediately and tell him you are a lady, and a lady does not receive mail in those sorts of envelopes!"

I wrote this information to Buck, who was stationed at Parris Island, South Carolina, and his letters arrived in undecorated envelopes thereafter. But there was nothing I could do to prevent the arrival of his birthday present to me, which came in a very large (undecorated) box. When I unwrapped the paper up in my room, and cut through the sealed tape, I found an enormous royal-blue satin pillow, with gold fringes and white tassels, and gold letters running its length announcing:

I'M A MARINE'S SWEETHEART

with a big red felt rose hanging above the words.

There was nothing to do but sneak it across to church the very next Sunday morning, and place it in Ape's pew, for her to find when she made her customary arrival, after nearly everyone from the town and the school was already seated.

Agnes and I had alienated almost everyone among the girls because we lived so far from them, and we were so often being disciplined. We became like the prisoners in the tower of some enormous castle, off by ourselves and all but forgotten except by Miss Woodland, who sometimes looked in on us . . . and Jan Fox.

When Agnes and I were at a point when we couldn't even go to the school-run tea shop, to get ourselves a box of Lorna Doones or vanilla wafers, Jan Fox came trundling down with contraband from her own closet. Tootsie Rolls, Baby Ruths, and Ritz crackers with little jars of Borden's pimento cheese, Kraft cheddar, and bacon and horseradish, plus Skippy creamy peanut butter and Welch's grape jam.

There was also a package of Old Gold cigarettes.

Agnes was allergic to cigarette smoke. When she saw the package, she went through the familiar motion signifying her displeasure: She held her nose with one hand, and reached up as though she was pulling a chain on an old-fashioned toilet.

"She can be our lookout if she's allergic to smoke," Jan said.

"How can we have a deaf lookout? She can't hear anyone coming and she can't let us know."

That comment got me a good punch in the arm from Agnes, who was watching everything I said.

She began pointing to herself and shaking her head up and down. She could so be a lookout!

If Miss Woodland came around the corner, not only could she shout out "Timber," but she could distract Miss Woodland, pretend to be sick or something. Miss Woodland was always overly solicitous of Agnes.

"She can do it!" Jan said.

"I don't know," I said. The truth was, I was hanging back because cigarettes made me dizzy and sick to my stomach, and I was already so deeply in trouble that being caught smoking would be the last straw. I'd be kicked out.

Agnes began to demonstrate how she'd warn us Timber was near.

"HIMMMM-HER! HIMMMMMM-HER!" was the way it came out.

"That's good enough!" said Jan.

Then Agnes showed us how she'd hold her stomach and pretend to need help across the hall to the bathroom.

"Perfect!" Jan said. "I never felt safe smoking down in my room."

"Perfect," I said weakly.

Jan decided we'd do it at night, after the lights-out bell, because we couldn't take the chance during the day, with practicing students on Middle Music.

That began an almost nightly tradition of Midnight Smoke And Eat Feasts.

It began near Easter, about two weeks before Easter Vacation, and I told myself if we could just survive until vacation, I'd come back from vacation with some excuse so I wouldn't have to smoke anymore. . . . Maybe I'd invent a doctor who'd tell me he'd discovered a strange fluxation in my lungs during a routine checkup . . . and just to be on the safe side, I'd nix smoking from there on in.

From my window, on moonlit nights, we had a good view of the faculty coming and going to movies, to meetings of the Red Cross in town, to whatever they went to for diversion.

We'd fix crackers in the closet by the light there, then take them over to my bed and watch what we could see—if not the teachers, then Mrs. Hodges tucking in her husband, Billy, a man much smaller than she was and not well, whose room was in a wing of Main across from me.

Agnes would join us for small periods of time, when the smoking was over.

The smoking was always first, and I always pretended to smoke more than I did, but the little tiny bit I had was enough to take my appetite away, and I never really enjoyed the food, either.

The ritual, I adored. One half hour after the lights-out bell, Jan Fox came sneaking through the halls, up the stairs from her room, with me watching from my doorway, and Agnes all the way out in the hall, since she could claim she hadn't heard the bell.

Although we called them Midnight Feasts, they usually got underway about ten-thirty, and ended a little after midnight.

They were also the occasion for our kissing games.

"Imagine that I'm Billy and you're Ape," Jan would say. "Come over to kiss me good night."

"Knotty-not, Bee-lee," I'd say, as close to Ape's thick southern accent as I could manage. I'd bend down and kiss Jan, and she'd always think of something "tawdry" to do—slurp my face with her tongue, bite my lip, flick her tongue up in my nostril. I'd draw back and say, "Bee-ly! Bee-ly! Bee-*lee! How taw-dree!*"

Then we'd collapse laughing.

Agnes would be Miss Woodland, surprised as she was kneeling by her bed in prayer. I'd be Billy, sneaking up behind her to put my arms around her, planting a wet kiss across her neck. Then Jan and I would pounce on Agnes to keep her sounds from being heard.

Everyone in the school knew two of the teachers were lesbians. They went everywhere together, and when they had a fight, they were as liable to have it by the drinking fountain outside Main study hall as anywhere, or at the dining table, in plain view, one ripping up the other's picture, one accusing the other of something. They looked the way you'd always think lesbians would look: one more masculine, almost totally male-looking until you saw the skirt, stockings, and oxfords . . . the other very feminine. The masculine one was always telling us, "Push yourself!" . . . The feminine one, a very southern lady, easily rattled, was always crying out, "I'm just sick in bed about this, girls."

We had our games of being these two teachers kissing, one of us mooning at the other, "I am sick in bed about you, darling," while the other embraced her saying, "Push yourself!"

On and on.

We felt like a very wonderful, witty, fast, tight triumvirate.

I even forgot to invent a doctor who'd found fluxations in my lung at Easter, but we were more interested in our games, eventually, than in Old Golds or Kraft cheese products.

Our triumvirate was to be ended forever the first week in June. Jan Fox was graduating.

The morning of graduation, parents descended on the campus, among them Jan Fox's glamorous mother, in a slinky white dress, with shoulder-length golden hair, under an enormous white straw picture hat.

Room campused even on that last day, Agnes and I watched the excitement from our windows, until it was time for Miss Woodland to escort us to the ceremony.

Miss Woodland joined the faculty, and we sat with the other students, waiting expectantly. Wearing white, and carrying red roses tied with large red-ribbon bows, the seniors marched into the gymnasium to "Pomp and Circumstance," under crooks decorated with daisies and ferns and carried by their ushers.

At the sight of Jan Fox, Agnes drew in her breath, and as I glanced at her, I saw tears starting to leak from her eyes.

She wiped them away while the commencement speaker stood at the podium.

Dramatically, he ripped the pages he was carrying in half, and said that nothing he had prepared to say would do for this day.

He said that this day would live in the memory of the world as a victorious and glorious day of triumph.

Agnes read it from his lips, stuck her elbow into my ribs, and put her hand across her mouth. Others were looking around in wonder at his words, frowning, suppressing laughter, nudging each other, raising eyes to the sky.

We had heard effusion aplenty from the pulpit, the study hall platform, and even the classroom, but this orator was kidding . . . wasn't he? We gave each other looks.

"Our boys," he went on, "fought for this day!"

Gradually we began to accept that it was just some sort of craziness unleashed on our particular seniors, a man who'd maybe never had a chance to speak to any class before, and had gone overboard in the heady excitement of his own personal appearance.

Many of us just concentrated on anything but what he was saying, to keep from laughing.

"This day will never, never be forgotten!"

I don't think two students present knew that under the supreme command of General Dwight D. Eisenhower, the Allies were invading Europe and establishing beachheads in Normandy, France.

Even as he went on, and we began to perceive that June 6, 1944, had a larger meaning for the world than Stuart Hall's graduation, we were not aware of what D-Day meant. No radio had prepared us; no news had filtered down to our cloister.

Perhaps the faculty appreciated the moment; they stayed stolid, in a block.

Listed as next on our programs was "The Alphabet, attributed to W. A. Mozart," performed by the Glee Club. It was during this, while Jan Fox sat up on the platform facing us, all in white with her red roses on her lap, that Agnes broke.

Her sentimental sobs thundered out of her at around "G" in the alphabet, and were loosened through most of the letters before "R," when she was finally gotten out of the place by a faculty member, so the ceremony could continue.

"Did I sound awful?" she wrote to me later, while we waited in our rooms for train time.

"You were the big hit of the day!" I said, and we both cried and laughed and finished packing.

"Damnation, can't someone even graduate with dignity!" Jan Fox appeared in the doorway, a crooked smile tipping her lips, an Old Gold caught between them, smoke wafting up past her face. She was there to say good-bye and give us roses from her bouquet, complaining that her mother was "bombed and ruining the parents' reception," hugging us, and hurrying from Middle Music, Hard Times, forever.

"I'll see you next year," I told Agnes when it was finally time for me to go and get my train.

"Heck here," Agnes said. "Guy!"

"Guy!"

"Guy! Guy! Guy!"

"Good-bye," I said, and it really was, because she didn't come back to school.

That night on the train I read *Life* magazine and got ready to reenter the real world.

Don't come to
San Francisco NOW

We want you to enjoy San Francisco when you come. This city and its region are too busy and crowded now to entertain you. War workers and Army and Navy personnel are taxing to capacity our hotels, housing, restaurants, transportation, and other facilities. Unless your need is imperative, please do not come to the San Francisco Bay area until the war is won.

and

Who'll help a hero home?

YOU will—if you'll just go easy on nonessential traveling. That will leave more Pullman beds for those who really need them. For civilians on war jobs. For soldiers going home before they go abroad. And for soldiers coming home—with rainbows on their chests.

Chris-Craft motorboat ads promised super deluxe cruisers

Ready after Victory. . . . We are 100% war work now.

The National Broadcasting Company promised that one day we would *watch* as well as hear our favorite shows.

Already, plans—within the limitations imposed by wartime— have been placed in operation by NBC . . . plans which with the cooperation of business and government will result in extensive NBC television networks . . . chains spreading from Eastern, Midwestern, and Western centers . . . gradually providing television after the war, to all the nation.

All the advertisements, from Beautyrest mattresses to Regal shoes to Johnnie Walker whiskey, declared,

BUY MORE WAR BONDS!

Around me, on the train, servicemen were everywhere, flirting, passing bottles, sleeping, sitting on baggage in the aisles, standing (one, not much older than I was, vomiting out a window) and singing songs like:

Roll me over,
Yankee soldier,
Roll me over,
Lay me down,
And do it again!

and

Bless 'em all,
Bless 'em all,
The long and the short and the tall,
It's sweet peas and violets,
For flat-footed pilots,
So God bless 'em all, bless 'em all!

When I got home, I found out that my kid brother, Butch, knew more about the war than I did. On a large map of the world in our basement, he and my father had tracked with pins everything from the battle in North Africa to the taking of islands in the Pacific, the invasions of Sicily, Netherlands New Guinea, the bombing of Berlin, the evacuation of Cassino—it was all there, for my four-year-old brother to explain to me.

My older brother was an ensign in the Navy, and as I sneaked a look at my father's journal, I came upon a description of a last night they spent together before "Junior" joined his carrier to fly in "Torpedo-9—famous in the battle of Midway."

I go as far as Chicago with him, where we check into the Stevens hotel. Lunch at 3:00 P.M. Sat the Pump Room, drinks at the Crystal Bar, the Morrison, and the Boulevard Tavern at the Stevens. We finally had supper together at a lunch counter where, when I realized it was the last meal I would ever have with my boy—as a boy—tears briefly got the better of me. We walked back to the Stevens. I helped him carry his grips downstairs, and on the sidewalk in front of the hotel, I told him to "take care of yourself." It was the best advice I could give him. We shook hands. He got in the airport bus and was gone. I had to walk the streets for thirty minutes, to gain control again of my emotions.

Agnes Thatcher was not her real name, and I did not know her as long as I knew other boarding school classmates. But I remembered her more, and featured her in my book *Is That You, Miss Blue?*

In that book I erroneously described her as "deaf and dumb," and I received mail correcting me. She was not "dumb," and that description of a deaf person is not appreciated.

Although we exchanged many notes, I apparently did not pay careful attention to hers. One of my favorite letters concerning that book was from a relative of a deaf person, who pointed out that my version of Agnes' notes did not ring true. "They are just not typical deaf letters," she said, "and although you caught many other things very well, the way you had her write was not the way someone deaf writes."

I'll comment more on my use of boarding school experiences later in this book.

Right now I just want to say that my interest in preachers' kids probably started when I roomed with Kay Walters, the first P.K. I ever really knew.

Preachers' kids figure in *Is That You, Miss Blue?* and are the main characters in *What I Really Think of You.*

In my book *Little Little*, a young evangelist preacher is featured who is also a dwarf, and the grandfather of the main character is a preacher.

While I came from a religious background (with one aunt who was a Roman Catholic nun) and attended an Episcopal boarding school, I always seemed to have a quarrel with organized religion.

I suppose the reason was simply that I always had a quarrel with authority of any kind.

I remember visiting Kay Walters' family in Sayre, Pennsylvania, one vacation from Stuart Hall, and announcing to her father that I was an atheist. I tried very hard to persuade Kay to declare herself an atheist while we were there. When I hinted at the idea, Reverend Walters said there was no reason, then, for either of us to go to his church for Sunday services. He took my pronouncements in good spirits, shrugging and smiling, and not giving me the fight I was probably looking for.

At the clanging of the church bell, Kay decided she really wasn't in my camp, and went along to church, as she always had, with her family—leaving me back at their house, abandoned and lonely in my "avowed atheism."

The event was described in *Is That You, Miss Blue?* though the character, Cardmaker, was based on an Army brat I knew and not on Kay. Like all true experiences that are later translated into fiction, some of it was that way, some of it wasn't that way, and sometimes the author no longer remembers what was and what wasn't.

Religion still fascinates me, whether it's a book by Paul Tillich, a local church service, a seder I'm invited to by Jewish friends, a talk with a Moonie on the street, a Billy Graham appearance, or one of the Sunday-morning TV preachers. I don't yet "believe"—and some of what I see I love or hate, but I'm rarely indifferent, which leaves me more involved than not.

Six:
Your Daddy Was a Sailor

The summer of 1944 I became Eric Ranthram McKay.

I think one reason for this was all the sailors pouring into our small town. There were some soldiers and marines around, too, but we knew them. They were hometown boys, coming and going from war. The sailors were another matter. On leave from nearby Sampson Naval Base, they came to us fresh from boot camp, lonely and looking for fun.

"The kind of fun a sailor is looking for might fill a few empty hours for him, but you could pay for it the rest of your life," my father said.

My mother even had a theory that "certain types" became

sailors: "The wolf types are attracted to that uniform," said she.

The sailors were no small consideration when my family decided to buy a cottage on Owasco Lake, at Burtis Point (the farthest point from town), and move there for the summer.

There, at the beginning of the summer, I was marooned. My father drove into work every morning at seven, and returned at six every evening. Gas rationing made it hard for anyone to get to and from Burtis Point. There were no buses. Hitchhikers didn't fare well on the empty roads at night, which discouraged local boyfriends from visiting. "Life" was going on back in town, at the movies, at the Teen Canteen and the USO, at the kids' hangouts like Murray's.

By day I swam and sailed and looked after my kid brother, listening to my girl friends' accounts of what was happening, for hours on the telephone. By night I wrote, using my first pseudonym: Eric Ranthram McKay.

The pseudonym was chosen because my father's initials were E. R. M. After I wrote a story, I mailed it off to a magazine with a letter written on my father's stationery, engraved with his initials and our home address.

I don't know why I chose Eric, Ranthram, or McKay—I guess I just felt the name had a good ring to it.

All of Eric Ranthram McKay's stories were sad, romantic ones about the war. I subscribed to a magazine called *Writer's Digest*, which listed the needs of publications like *Good Housekeeping*, *Ladies' Home Journal*, and *Redbook*. I mailed off my stories in manila envelopes with a stamped, addressed envelope enclosed, and they came back like boomerangs, with printed rejection slips attached.

Sometimes these rejection slips had a "sorry" penciled across them, or a "try again."

Those I cherished, and saved, and used to buoy my spirits as I began new stories, and kept the old ones circulating.

At the same time Eric Ranthram McKay was writing stories, Marijane Meaker was writing servicemen—a soldier named Bob McKeon from my hometown, and a sailor named Eddie Herbold. Herbold was considered an okay sailor, since my family knew him. These "romances," by mail, were in full swing that summer.

Nights when my father arrived at the cottage with the mail, he always tried to soften the blow of a new rejection (there was often one of my self-addressed stamped envelopes in the pile) by calling out, "Herbold came through!" or "McKeon came through!" handing me one of their letters first.

Scotch-taped around my bureau mirror were pictures of Bob and Eddie, and rejection slips with a few blunt words written on them.

One story, "Your Daddy Was a Sailor," came back with the single word "Touching" written across the rejection slip.

I carried that rejection slip with me everywhere in the back pocket of my jeans.

"Your Daddy Was a Sailor" was about a girl from a small town who was warned by her parents never to date a sailor. She fell in love with one she met at a church dance. "Where did you meet this *sailor*?" her mother demanded. "I met him at church," Evelyn answered. "Reverend Lathrop introduced us." . . . Since she met him at church, she was allowed to see him. . . . But forget church; he was a sailor, wasn't he? So the inevitable happened, on a night with "stars twinkling like diamonds overhead, and the next day he would go off to fight, maybe never to return."

Skip to the future, and a woman living in a big city far from her hometown, working and raising her little boy by herself. She remembers the small town she had to leave when she became pregnant, and the quiet summer nights there, while outside her windows are the honking horns of big-city traffic. She wonders about her family, whom she hasn't seen in so long. She reads and rereads an old "last letter," a love letter from a Pacific island (suspiciously like one of Eddie Herbold's to Marijane Meaker), and then she picks up her little boy, hugs him close, and says, "Your daddy was a sailor!"

After my own father read the story, he said, "You better rewrite it and make it clear the sailor died."

"You know he died," I said. "She was rereading the last letter."

"A last letter could mean he skipped out on her. When a girl gets in trouble, more skip out than die."

In those days, when people said a girl was "in trouble," that meant only one thing: She was pregnant and unmarried.

While nobody ever described the boy as being "in trouble," he was, if he was from the same town. He usually had to marry the girl, whether he wanted to or not.

Couples who found themselves in that situation had "shotgun weddings"—so called from an old hillbilly custom in which the father of the girl would point a shotgun at the boy's head until the knot was tied.

Eric Ranthram McKay also wrote a story about a shotgun wedding, called "Country Club Boy." It dealt with a poor girl in a small town, who got pregnant during a wartime affair with a rich boy. They had to marry, and when he was shipped overseas, his mother was embarrassed to introduce her as "my daughter-in-law" at the country club. . . . That story was gleaned from telephone gossip about a local girl, not in our crowd, who had a shotgun wedding with a boy we all knew, and moved in with his family, pregnant and none too welcome there.

Eric Ranthram McKay began to bother my mother.

It wasn't natural for a young girl to be closeted in a cottage bedroom night after night of a summer, writing such stories. "You need to get your mind off all that writing," my mother complained to me.

She told my father, "She doesn't want to talk with us, or play Monopoly, or listen to the radio, or do anything but stay up there by herself in her dream world, writing."

I liked being Eric Ranthram McKay, but I was restless, too.

Finally, a deal was worked out with my father. I would get a summer job in town, and he would buy me a secondhand car so I could drive back and forth to work.

In mid-July I became the owner of a 1935 LaSalle convertible, complete with rumble seat in the back (it cost him two hundred dollars), and I became employed as an operator for the telephone company.

This was a job that delighted me. Although I didn't do anything but sit in front of a switchboard, push and pull plugs, and say "Number please?" and "Thank you," I soon found out how to listen in on conversations.

Not only could I hear my girl friends gossiping, I could hear my own mother giving out her version of our family life to friends.

I discovered that she suspected my father of having an affair with his secretary.

I discovered that she had decided to have my little brother to keep my father interested in a homelife, after my older brother and I were grown.

I also discovered that she thought I wrote so much because I was self-conscious about my long nose, that writing was my way of hiding.

Up until that moment, I hadn't thought my nose was all that long . . . and so I'd been given something to think about—obsess about—appropriate punishment, perhaps, for my snooping.

But I was back in the swing of things. I had a car, a little extra spending money (though I had to turn back some of my salary to my father, to help pay for the car), and access to the new hangout, Boysen's, as well as the old soda shop, Murray's.

Boysen's sold liquor, and even though we weren't old enough to drink, our crowd favored it because the older boys (18, 19) and servicemen hung out there.

We went from Murray's to Boysen's, and from Boysen's to Murray's, many of the girls dragging their knitting bags with them, sitting around in these places after work knitting and drinking Cokes, listening to the jukebox, greeting old faces in new uniforms, gossiping and watching and reading each other the lastest V-mail from boyfriends.

I began dating a boy named William Dougan Annan, who was blind in one eye and couldn't get into the service because of that. He was tall and blond, really good-looking (we said "sharp"—"Oh, is he sharp!"), and we started going steady, deciding on an old song, "Where or When," as our song. This courtship we gave each other silver identification brace- lets: His said *Where?*; mine said *When?*

On the day Paris was liberated, and General Eisenhower was planning his march into the French capital, I received a wire that Jan Fox was arriving for a visit.

"Jan Fox," I warned Dougan, "is the most sophisticated person I've ever met in my life, so we've got to fix her up with someone really sharp!

"Jan Fox," I warned my family, "is not from small-town people, so I just hope we're not going to behave like hicks around her."

"Shall we all dress every night for dinner?" my father said.

"It's not funny," I said. "Her father's this big corporate lawyer and her mother socializes in Palm Springs, places like that."

"We're not going to act any differently than we ever act," said my mother.

"I just wish we had such a thing as a cocktail hour around here," I said..

"We have the hour," my father said, "we just don't have the cocktail."

"She drinks martinis," I said.

"Not in this house," my mother said.

"She's practically eighteen!" I said.

"I'll put a ginger ale in a cocktail glass for her at five in the afternoon," said my mother.

"With an olive," my father said.

"She also smokes," I said.

My mother said, "Not in this house."

Jan Fox arrived late on a Friday afternoon, and no matter how I tried to get my mother to change her mind about it, we had the usual Friday-night dinner, a favorite of my father's: Boston baked beans, brown bread, and salad. Choice of beverage: milk or water.

"Of course, this isn't where we really live," I explained to Jan as she unpacked up in my bedroom. "This is just a shack we bought to come to summers, to rough it. When we're up here we always eat stuff people eat at the lake, nothing fancy," I went on, just as though we didn't have baked beans fifty-two Friday nights a year. "This is sort of a health thing for us in summer, you know, lots of exercise, no smoking, no drinking."

"Don't worry about it."

"That's why I bought that tacky car, too," I said (it was my pride and joy!), "to sort of get into the spirit of things, roughing it and all . . . and it's wartime, so we don't want to be ostentatious."

"Don't worry about it."

"We'll get going later," I promised. "Dougan's fixed you up with Murray Townsend. Murray's from out of town. His people summer here, on the other side of the lake."

Then we went down to dinner, both of us in heels and leg paint, in summer dresses, ready for our dates, who were picking us up at seven-thirty.

As my father dished up the beans, and passed a plate across to Jan, she said, "Beans, beans, the musical fruit, the more you eat, the more you toot!"

My father frowned while my mother blanched. Hiccuping was about the only untoward bodily function anyone in the family even admitted to, and anything that went on in the bathroom beyond bathing, shaving, or brushing your teeth was never acknowledged.

I laughed and laughed, because no one else did, and I hoped Jan Fox wouldn't notice that no one else did, while my mind whirled with disbelief that she'd said it.

Meanwhile, my mother was trying to give me the eye, to say with one long, hard look what all the vibrations from her body were already transmitting to me: the most sophisticated person you know?

After that, it wasn't so bad that my father picked up his fork and said, "Dig in," and my kid brother chewed with his mouth open.

I just figured we were all going downhill in a hand barrel, as my mother was fond of saying.

At seven-thirty sharp we were still lingering at the table, over coffee, while Jan talked about her ambition to be a lawyer. Then a horn honked.

"That's them!" I said. "Let's go!"

"Sit down," said my father, as Jan and I were starting to get up.

"Our dates are here, Dad."

"Sit . . . down."

We sat down.

Another honk of the horn.

"*Dad,*" I said, "it's Murray Townsend's car. Murray's driving. He doesn't know all your rules."

The horn honked again.

We sat there.

"What's the problem?" Jan asked me.

"They have to come in and kneel before the king."

"Marijane is a lady," said my father. "When she has gentlemen callers, they come to the door, knock, wait to be invited in, enter, speak with her parents, and then leave with her, assuming that her parents find them halfway respectable."

"I love it!" Jan laughed.

"*I,*" I said, "hate it!"

By that time Dougan was knocking at the screen door.

"Come in, Dougan," my father bellowed out, "and tell the drugstore cowboy behind the wheel of the car to get himself in here, too!"

I groaned.

"I love it!" Jan kept saying.

"Tell him to bring his driver's license in with him!" my father yelled after Dougan.

I wished I was Eric Ranthram McKay, back upstairs where I belonged, writing about life instead of enduring it.

Murray Townsend, a tall, sullen blond with big white teeth, was driving his father's new, white Buick convertible, top down, radio playing full blast, as we headed into town. Jan sat beside him and bummed a cigarette from him, while Dougan and I sat in back with the wind blowing fiercely in our faces.

"I think Murray's pretty p.o.'d at your dad," Dougan told me.

"You should have warned him," I said. "It's not my fault he's that way."

"He talked to him like he was a kid. Murray's eighteen. He's going to be a doctor."

"Jan's going to be a lawyer," I said. "What do you think of her?"

Dougan shrugged. "She's all right."

"All right?" I said. "Just wait. She's sharp."

We all went to see *I'll Be Seeing You.*

Joseph Cotton played a wounded vet on furlough, who fell in love with a convicted killer, Ginger Rogers. She'd pushed her boss out of a window after he made a pass at her, and she was on Christmas leave from the peniten-tiary

Jan and I both cried whenever the title tune came on the soundtrack, and at the end, but Murray said it was another silly wartime movie as we walked down to Boysen's.

I'd already warned Dougan that I wanted him to order me a real drink. In Boysen's everyone got their drinks from the bar. They rarely asked anyone at a table for proof of age, so long as the one stepping up to the bar could prove he was eighteen.

"What are you girls drinking?" Murray asked once we were settled in a booth, and I said, "Jan likes martinis."

"Oh, I don't know," Jan said, and I said, "She drinks them until they come out of her ears."

Murray said to Dougan, "And you two?"

"Tom Collins," said Dougan.

Boysen's was packed with the usual mixture of our crowd, servicemen, sailors from Sampson, and girls from the older crowd, still in their coveralls, coming off a shift at one of the local defense plants.

The jukebox was playing songs like "I'll Walk Alone" and "Don't Get Around Much Anymore" and "Saturday Night Is the Loneliest Night in the Week."

There was a very red-cheeked, baby-faced sailor feeding it quarters, and Jan nicknamed him "Sad Eyes" a short while after she'd downed her first martini.

When she got up to help him make some selections, Murray said to me, "I thought she was supposed to be sophisticated."

"She *is*," I said.

"She doesn't even inhale," he said. "Why does she smoke if she doesn't even inhale?"

"She inhales!" I said. "*Jan?* She smokes like a chimney."

"She doesn't inhale," Dougan said.

"She drinks martinis at ten o'clock at night!" Murray said.

"What's that got to do with anything?"

Dougan said, "You drink martinis *before* dinner, not after."

"What do *you* know about martinis?" I said.

"I know what Murray told me."

"Exactly!" I said. "You're both just ganging up on her because I said she was sophisticated, and she is."

"She's got you snowed," Murray said.

"You're just teed off because she's paying attention to that cute sailor."

"I don't care who she pays attention to," Murray said. "I'm just doing Dougan a favor."

"I think she's already tipsy," Dougan said.

"On *one* martini?" I said. "She drinks them until they come out of her ears!"

"She's fried right now," said Murray.

When Jan and I went to the ladies' together, I said, "Are you all right?"

"What do you mean am I all right?"

"Nothing," I said.

"I just can't stand that hick you fixed me up with. He looks like a chipmunk."

"It's just for one night," I said.

"I like Sad Eyes better. At least he's not a slacker."

"Murray's not a slacker. He's going to be a doctor. He's going into V-Twelve."

"I like Dougan all right, but my date's a bore. It's not *your* fault."

"I tried."

"You tried," she agreed, "and thanks for trying." She pronounced it "twying" and stepped back in a sudden little lurch.

"Are you okay?"

"What's the matter with you?" she said.

We had two more rounds before we left Boysen's to make my father's one-o'clock curfew.

On the way home, we had to stop the car while she got sick.

When we got to the cottage, my father was out on the screen porch reading *A Bell for Adano* and smoking his pipe. My mother was in bed, asleep. Pale-faced and shaky, Jan went up to my room.

"Where's your friend?" my father said.

"She's dead tired," I said. "She said to say good night."

"Where did you go?"

"To the movies, to Murray's," I said. "The usual."

"That boy you fixed her up with looks like a chipmunk," said my father.

The next day I discovered that Ellis Robert Meaker fascinated Jan far more than Eric Ranthram McKay did.

Instead of reading my stories, she swam out to the raft in front of our cottage with my father, and sat in the sun with him talking for hours.

"I thought that little remark of hers about musical fruit was in very poor taste," said my mother as we watched them from the lawn.

"She never says things like that," I said. "She was just recovering from the shock of being served baked beans for dinner."

"Why hasn't anyone from her family called to see that she got here all right?"

"I don't know," I said. "Ask her—no, don't," I said.

"It's very strange, a young girl traveling alone."

"Her parents are divorced," I said.

"One of them must care about what happens to her."

"Muth-*ther*," I said, "they're not small-town people. She travels all the time, probably, all over the world, probably."

"She doesn't even carry a plate to the kitchen. Did she help you make the bed this morning?"

I decided not to answer.

"I bet she didn't," my mother said.

When they finally came in from the raft, after Jan went up to change out of her bathing suit, my father said, "You could learn something from her."

"Like?"

"Like thinking about a profession for yourself, since you want to go to college."

"I'm going to be a writer."

"That's not a profession, Marijane, that's a way to starve. Now, Jan has her eye on the law as a profession. A lawyer can always make money, even a bad lawyer can make money. Writing is a nice hobby, but you can't earn a living writing. There aren't any degrees in writing."

"There are in journalism," I said.

"Journalism isn't a real profession," said my father. "I'm talking about a *profession*. Jan has a head on her shoulders. She's planning her future very carefully."

"Well, I'm glad someone in the family likes her," I said.

"She wants to be a corporate lawyer. Now that's a good choice. There're not many women in the field, and she's a looker, so she'll wrap those corporation people around her little finger."

"Like she has you," I said.

"Well, she's a nice, intelligent girl, with those long legs—she'll get someplace."

Right before my mother served lunch, the phone rang, and the caller asked for Jan.

"Well, it's about time," said my mother. "Her family *waited* long enough."

After lunch, Jan and I took a walk up the beach.

"That was Sad Eyes who called," she said. "He wants a date with me, and he's got a sailor for you."

"Are you kidding? My father'd kill me!"

"Why?"

"Because I can't date strange sailors. You just met him last night in Boysen's. How'm I going to explain that to my father?"

"Can't we say we're going somewhere by ourselves tonight?"

"We don't even know them, Jan!"

"Look, his name is Charlie Kelly. He's really nice. Can't we figure out something? Are you a prisoner of your family?"

"I suppose we can figure out something."

"We can take your car, can't we?"

"I suppose."

"It'll be fun!" she said.

. . . *The kind of fun a sailor is looking for might fill a few empty hours for him* . . . my father's baleful warning echoed in my ears, *but you could pay for it,* et cetera et cetera.

I told Dougan that Jan didn't want to go out that night, and Dougan said he wasn't surprised, she was probably still hung over.

"That means we can't go into town," I told Jan, "because Dougan will see us."

"What about your house?" Jan said. "Don't you have a key to your house?"

"The neighbors would call my mother if they saw lights on, and my car, and sailors."

"There has to be some way we could get in without them seeing the sailors. You could say you were showing me the house. I want to see it."

"What would we do there?"

"Haven't you got a phonograph, some records? We could just have a party. I don't want to drink after last night, but we could just fool around."

"What did they say they wanted to do?"

"They're from out of town. They're just these lonely guys. We'll just play records, dance—have a party!"

"Oh, I don't know," I said, but I was already figuring out that we could park my car on Marvin Avenue, go up through the fields, go in the cellar door, and have the party down there in the rec room, where there were no windows neighbors could see lights in.

I was vacillating until Jan said, "And you know what I want to do this afternoon? I want to sit down somewhere by myself and read every one of your stories!"

She always seemed to know how to get to me.

The Wacs and Waves are winning the war,
Parlez-vous,
The Wacs and Waves are winning the war,
Parlez-vous,
The Wacs and Waves are winning the war,
So what the hell are we fighting for?
Hinky, dinky, parlez-vous.

We were a motley crew.

Instead of there being two sailors, there were three: Charlie, with the baby face and sad blue eyes; Dino, with tight, black curly hair, who pronounced "bottle" "bot-ul" and was from Brooklyn, New York; Tub, who was short and very fat, perspiring and begging me for more air in our muggy, hot basement.

They brought bags of bottled beer and Cokes, pretzels and potato chips, salami and cheese and crackers.

Our rec room was decorated with World War I memorabilia, photos of my father's days in the American field corps of the French army.

The furniture was yellow wicker with bright-green cushions that smelled of mildew, and there were skis, sleds, a toboggan, bicycles, and ice skates piled around, a rolled-up dusty carpet running the length of the room, and a very old stand-up phonograph you had to crank to work. I took a flashlight up to my room, to bring down some of my records, but there wasn't much room to dance, and we got tired of winding up the machine.

We drank beer and sang and ate by candlelight, and Dino

did imitations: President Roosevelt, James Cagney, Eleanor Roosevelt, Bing Crosby, on and on.

The most sophisticated person I had ever met in my entire life had turned into a blushing, giggling schoolgirl who was letting Charlie show her a new way to drink beer. He'd get a mouthful, then put his mouth against hers, open it, and let it trickle down her throat.

Dino got into a heartfelt imitation of Frank Sinatra singing "I'll Never Smile Again," and Tub was wandering around in my father's workshop, in the next room, hoping for more air, running his fingers along the edges of my father's buzz saw and saying things like "Hey, these things could take your fingers off!"

We were there for hours, long, long hours that dragged by—I kept looking at my watch, not just because of my usual one-o'clock curfew, but because I couldn't believe sixty minutes lasted twenty-four hours; yet we were there for days, like the man who spent a year in Philadelphia one night.

My mouth really hurt from smiling smiles I didn't feel like smiling, though I couldn't let on to poor Dino that another imitation and I'd scream. Tub's white sailor suit was soaked, under his arms and all down his back, and he was beginning to smell, even from the other room.

My only consolation was that Jan Fox seemed to be having the time of her life, but that consolation was deeply depressing, and I kept thinking of the chipmunk telling me she'd had me snowed.

I know exactly the point DOOM descended.

Charlie and Jan were drinking beer from each other's mouths on the wicker couch. Tub was sitting on the rolled-up rug mopping his forehead with a large, square, white handkerchief. Dino, the Indefatigable Entertainer, was doing another imitation: ". . . This is Bob-broadcasting-to-you-from-Camp Crowder-Hope, saying—" when my father came through the basement door.

He stood there, pointing the way he'd come, barking, "OUT!"

I remember mumbling something about the boys having no way to get home and not even knowing where they were.

"OUT! OUT! OUT!" he persisted, and out they went, into the night, never to be seen or heard from again.

Jan and I cleaned up after ourselves in a silence so heavy you would have had to cut it with some sharp electrical thing from the other room. My father waited, his face like a storm cloud ready to crack along with thunder and lightning.

As we headed out to his car, I managed to say, "My car's down on Marvin Avenue."

"So nearly everyone on Marvin Avenue said," he told me. "Our phone hasn't stopped ringing. You locked the door and left your lights on!"

Then he said, "The motor's probably dead anyway. We'll stop and turn off the lights, and you can get it tomorrow when—"

"We didn't mean anything wrong, Mr. Meaker." Jan tried to calm him down.

"Tomorrow," my father continued, "when we're on the way to the train Jan is catching."

We drove back to Burtis Point in silence, except for the sound of hiccups from Jan Fox and one solitary, under-the-breath remark from my father: "Sailors!"

I corresponded with Jan Fox for a while, and then lost track of her.

Before I went away to boarding school, I always thought I was a rich kid. I always thought my family was really sophisticated.

Jan Fox, and the boarding school experience, got me thinking twice about this, and for the first time I began to meet kids who made me feel like the small-town girl I really was.

I went through a period during which I decided my family were really these awful hicks, nothing but an embarrassment to me. Why did my mother wear so much junk jewelry? Why did my father have to say things like "Soup's on!" instead of "Dinner's ready," or "How do?" instead of "How do you do?" Why did my mother have to mention the price of everything, and talk about "bargains"? Why didn't we ever have wine with dinner, or go to concerts, and why did my father have to call classical music "long-hair noise?"

Why didn't we collect art, ride horseback, have dinner parties, or serve cocktails?

I was very thankful I hadn't chosen a boarding school close to home, and that the war made it impossible for them to visit, because I was sure my family would just be a humiliation to me.

My family was probably wondering around the same time what they'd done wrong to produce this girl who called herself Eric Ranthram McKay.

Once I received a letter from a kid doing a paper on M. E. Kerr.

"Why did you decide to name your pen?" he asked me.

I don't think my father's ERM stationery was the sole reason I began writing under a pen name. I think I was drawn to the idea I could create this separate identity for myself, and write about people I knew without them ever knowing who was telling their secrets.

Since nearly all of my pseudonyms were male, I must have also felt that a female wouldn't be taken seriously.

Even when I finally talked my father into letting me go to journalism school, he argued that no matter whether or not the University of Missouri had a better school than the one in nearby Syracuse, New York, I should go to Syracuse.

"Why?" I asked him.

"Because if you go to Missouri," he said, "you'll marry a boy from Missouri. You'll live in Missouri. You'll never get back for holidays, and we'll see very little of you."

From his viewpoint, it wasn't *what* a girl studied, it was where. All college did was provide a place for you to meet your future husband.

Once, I toyed with the idea of becoming a librarian, since I loved libraries so much. I could work in a library and write on the side.

"That's a terrible idea," my father said. "If you go to library school, you'll never meet a man!"

Years and years later, I discovered I wasn't the only one who felt a female wouldn't be taken seriously. When I first began writing suspense stories for Fawcett Publications, my editor suggested that I take a male pseudonym.

"You tell a fast, tough story," he said, "and you'll lose your credibility with a name like Marijane Meaker."

I chose the pen name Vin Packer, after talking about the problem over dinner with one friend whose first name was Vin and another whose last name was Packer.

Even in the '60's, when I did a nonfiction book on suicide for Doubleday, called *Sudden Endings*, my editor suggested that I call myself M. J. Meaker, instead of Marijane Meaker.

"Marijane," she said, "isn't right for a book on suicide."

While I did do a few novels under my real name, I always felt better when I "named my pen."

When I named it M. E. Kerr, it was a play on my last name, and probably a hangover from the days when I felt, along with others, that a female writer wouldn't sell as well as a male would.

Seven:
What I Did
Between Trains

On my way back to boarding school after Christmas vacation, in January 1945, I had the usual long wait between trains.

There was no chaperone for vacation travel, no Jan Fox anymore—most of my classmates were southerners, so I was on my own.

I'd cruise the bookstores and novelty shops around 42nd Street, afraid to wander too far from Grand Central Station. Then I'd wedge myself into a seat in the station, which was teeming with travelers, mostly servicemen on furlough from camps in the south.

I had a leading role in the upcoming school play, *The Importance of Being Earnest*, by Oscar Wilde.

I'd sit for a while, memorizing my part, while Kate Smith sang "God Bless America" over the loudspeaker. Then I'd get up again and stroll around in the crowd.

I was to be Algernon Moncrieff in the play.

I'd sit, sandwiched between exhausted journeyers, going over and over Algernon's lines: "Why is it that at a bachelor's establishment the servants invariably drink the champagne?"

Soldiers and sailors would pass lugging barracks bags and suitcases, some with their wives and tired little screaming kids in tow.

I'd continue: "Good Heavens! Lane! Why are there no cucumber sandwiches? I ordered them specially!"

Through an elaborate code worked out between my brother and my father, we knew from his letters that he was on a carrier somewhere near the Admiralty Islands. It was our third Christmas without him.

There were nationwide dimouts now to conserve rapidly diminishing fuel supplies.

Soviet troops were liberating Auschwitz, where more than a million Jews had died in SS gas chambers.

Nonetheless, there I sat, concentrating on the business at hand: "No cucumbers! . . . I am greatly distressed, Aunt Augusta, about there being no cucumbers, not even for ready money!"

(My mother was not too happy about the fact I would don nineteenth-century drag to star in this comedy of manners.)

On one of my strolls outside the station, I wandered into a crowded little newsstand filled with magazines, toilet articles, packaged snacks, stationery, and toys. There I spotted a cork dartboard for sale.

On a whim, I decided to buy it and take it to my room at school. I was back in Robertson House with my class that year, sharing with my old P.K. roommate again.

Little did I know how much that dartboard would change the course of my senior year.

I had it wrapped, lugged it on and off the train to Washington, D.C., guarded it through another long wait in the station, got it aboard another train, and arrived with it, finally, in Virginia.

Before I hung it on a hook behind the door of our room, I decorated it.

I found an old school yearbook and cut out all the pictures of the faculty, placing their faces where numbers were, printing their nicknames carefully across their countenances.

There was "Beethoven" across Miss Stone's face, and "Timber" across Miss Woodland's, "No Tits" across Miss Lackbrest's, and "Chicken" across Miss Hennig's. Dead center, bull's-eye, was our headmistress, "Ape."

Life went on.

The school play was in rehearsal. All the seniors were applying to various colleges, mostly southern ones like Sweet Briar and Randolph-Macon. (I was trying for the University of Missouri, known for its Journalism School.)

Dougan and I were working on a plan for him to come down for a spring dance. The plan involved my scraping together enough money to go halves with him on the cost of a train ticket. I began writing compositions for my classmates, at three dollars apiece: "The Character of Hamlet," "The Athens of Sophocles," "Dryden's Odes Compared to Milton's," et cetera. . . . I also ran errands for a dollar.

There was the usual studying, writing to servicemen, on and on, except now there was a daily game of darts in our room on Robertson. I invited everyone to play. When the game was finished, I hid the dartboard way back in my closet, covering it with an old shoe bag.

Our rooms were inspected daily by Mrs. Needleman, our housemother—"Needle Eye, the Nazi Spy" known for her skill in ferreting out Hershey bars from the bottoms of Kotex boxes and reading all personal mail. (We would leave notes for her inside letters: "How are you today, dear Mrs. Needleman?")

February 22nd, appropriately on George Washington's birthday (he who would not tell a lie), I sat across from Ape, in her office, lying through my teeth.

"Holes?" I said. "What are you talking about?"

"What are you talking about, Mrs. Hodges?" she corrected me.

"What are you talking about, Mrs. Hodges?"

"I'm talking about the tiny little holes on the back of your door, as though someone deliberately took something like an icepick, and punctured the wood."

Not everyone had hit the dartboard every time; some of the darts had hit the door.

"Maybe it's some kind of insect," I said. "Termites, possibly."

"I want you to tell me how those holes got there."

"I don't know anything about any holes."

"They're new holes and it's your room."

"Holes?"

"If you don't tell me how they got there, I'll call Kay in here to see what she knows about them."

"Kay doesn't know anything about them."

"I don't doubt that."

"I mean, how would Kay know about them if I don't know about them?"

Ape was fingering the large pearls she always wore around her neck beneath her third chin. This was her habit before she blew up.

"If there *are* holes on the back of my door," I said, "I would be glad to fill them and paint over them. I can do that, if there are such holes."

Ape got to her feet. "We are going over to your room RIGHT NOW and look at those holes together."

"Why go all the way over there?" I said. I was trying to think how I could first get the pictures off the front of the dartboard, and then confess that I owned a dartboard. "I have to believe you, Mrs. Hodges, so why go all the way over there?"

"Because I *want* to go all the way over there, and I want *you* with me! You claim you've never noticed those holes. I want you to notice them in my presence!"

"Okay," I said desperately, still sitting down while she stood over me. "Okay. The holes were made by darts. Just darts. I have some darts."

A nerve was jumping under the skin on one side of Ape's face.

"They're just dart holes," I said.

"The holes go around in a circle," she said. "What was in that circle?"

I knew she knew then . . . everything.

Needle Eye, the Nazi Spy, had struck again.

"What was in that circle?" Ape persisted.

"Why don't you ask the person who went through my private closet?" I said.

"Why don't we both go and look at your private closet? RIGHT NOW!"

"All right. I have a dartboard. I'll go get it," I offered.

But I was a Yankee, facing defeat in Dixieland, as surely as General Lee had lost to us in 1865.

Ape yanked me to my feet. "Come along! We're going to go over there and get that dartboard right this minute. . . . Not only have you defaced school property," she continued as we crossed the thick carpet in her office, "but you have told a deliberate lie!"

That very night, four days from the opening of *The Importance of Being Earnest*, I was on the sleeper to New York City.

The next morning, between trains again in Grand Central Station, I wedged myself between a sailor and a sleeping Marine, and opened *The New York Times* to the want ads.

Mrs. Hodges had bought my train ticket, but I had thirty-three dollars with me, from my "Dougan's Train Ticket" fund.

I taxied to the Park Lane Hotel, where I filled out an application for a job as a switchboard operator. I enlarged a little on my experience at the phone company in my hometown. There was a war on, help was hard to find—I was told to come back the next day.

I stepped into a phone booth and called home, collect.

"Don't bother to meet my train in Syracuse," I told my father, surprised that he'd answered the phone, when he was supposed to be at his office. "I have a job. I'll write you. I'm not coming home."

"Now listen very carefully, sweetie pie," he said. "You catch your train to Syracuse, as planned. No one here is angry with you."

"What are you doing home?" I imagined him so upset at this new developement that he hadn't been able to go to work.

"Digging out," he said. "We had a big snowstorm last night. Come home and we'll get the toboggan out."

"I'm not even going to be a high school graduate now," I said.

"You can go to school here."

"You said if I wasn't asked back there, I couldn't continue school."

"You can continue school. We want you home."

"Is this a trick to get me home so you can really give it to me?"

"No. No one's going to give it to you."

"I can't face all the talk in town."

"We won't say you were expelled. We'll say you came home on your own."

"In the middle of the semester? No one's going to believe that. I can't face all the talk."

"Just remember what P. T. Barnum said," my father said. "P. T. Barnum said, 'I don't care what they say, so long as they talk.' "

I could see a young corporal outside the phone booth, waiting for me to finish.

"Is this a trick?" I said.

"No. I can't wait to see you! Okay?"

"What does *she* think about it?" I said.

"Your mother's relieved," he said.

"Relieved?"

"That you're not going to play a man in the school play," he said. "Come on home!"

2/23/45—Marijane is expelled for lying to Mrs. Hodges [my father wrote in his journal]. *Trumped-up charge! They never got along. We are going to fight it! Meanwhile she must get a job.*

From the end of February through March, I worked in the office of American Locomotive, a local defense plant, as a file clerk. Meanwhile, my mother and father made phone calls and wrote letters to Ape, Father J. Lewis Gibbs, chaplain of the school, and various southern Episcopal bishops.

I told everyone but Dougan the school had an extra-long Easter vacation, to conserve fuel, though I doubt many people really believed that.

But in April I was back, Ape warning me that "one false move and nothing will save you! And anyway, there'll be no recommendation from this office for any college you make application to!"

Somehow I was graduated, two months before President

Truman proclaimed V-J day, and the end of World War II.

In the school yearbook, *Inlook*, 1945, I am distinctively out of place, since it was put together during my expulsion. At the very end of the seniors' photographs comes Kathryn Walters, my roommate; then Wellford, Worthy and Yates . . . then Marijane Meaker, on record forever, the out-of-line black sheep.

In my teens I was always "the bad kid"—my grades were bad, and I was "bad."

No one could have ever convinced me then that one day the boarding school I'd attended—and nearly gotten permanently expelled from—would ask me to write something for their *Bulletin/ Catalog*, but that's what happened.

It was published in 1977, under the heading: STUART HALL GRADUATES, along with my picture.

Author
Marijane Meaker, '45
I think my years at Stuart Hall were a provocative experience for both Stuart Hall and me. I was the class reprobate, assigned a single room the size of a large closet on Middle Music Hall to keep me out of trouble. Nevertheless, I was very familiar with Mrs. Hodges' office, where I would go after finding in my mailbox, many a morning, a note exclaiming, "See me at once! APH." . . . In my senior year I was expelled, and only my mother's intervention with a bishop had that changed to a suspension, so I could return to graduate

*with my class. . . . I had, while I was there, and well after,
a great infatuation with Stuart Hall, a lover's quarrel with
its rules and certain stern faculty members, and now I read
it's changed and not so strict, and wonder would I love it
so well these days? I don't know, but there was something
stimulating and amusing, and very like life, as I came to
know it, in its regulated, intense, dutiful and peculiar ambi-
ance. I went there during World War II, and I remember so
well getting there on overcrowded trains jammed with boys
just a few years older than I, on their way to war. Many of
us had brothers away at war. It was a difficult time . . .
and I remember Mrs. Hodges calling an assembly to announce Roosevelt's death, and dear Miss Dean, the science
teacher, correcting her former opinion that atoms could not
be split.*

The first story I ever sold was about Stuart Hall. The
Ladies' Home Journal *bought it, launching me on my writing
career in 1950, one year after I'd graduated from the University of Missouri, where I went to study journalism. I had never
wanted to be anything but a writer. . . . My first book, too,
was about Stuart Hall. I called it* Catalog on Request. *It was
rejected everywhere. So I'm delighted that now* Is That You,
Miss Blue? *is published; it is fiction about a favorite place,
under one of my pseudonyms, M. E. Kerr (a play on my
last name). I've written many suspense books under the
name Vin Packer, several books under my own name, includ-
ing my favorite,* Shockproof Sydney Skate, *a 1972 Literary
Guild Selection. My latest,* I'll Love You When You're More
Like Me, *another M. E. Kerr published by Harper & Row,
will come out Fall, 1977.*

It's my wish that every "bad kid" out there will one day get the same chance to look good, years and years later.

One of the criticisms leveled at *Is That You, Miss Blue?* came from a Stuart Hall student in 1976. She said some of the story was spoiled for her because "today's boarding schools just aren't that strict."

I think that's a good criticism, and it pointed out a flaw in the book.

When I take an experience from the past and put it into the present, I work hard to update it. I guess where Stuart Hall was concerned, I just couldn't make the jump. Boys on campus at Stuart Hall? Trips to town unchaperoned? Weekends away from school? . . . Surely if I had written it that way, I would have found a note in my mailbox saying, "See me at once! APH!"

Eight:
The Sister of
Someone Famous

Vermont Junior College had decided to take a chance on me. That was the way the dean put it. She was a woman named Ruth Kingsley, whose personality was as far removed from Ape's as Athene's is from Hecate's.

"I know my grades weren't very good," I told Dean Kingsley.

"Your grades were the least of it," she answered. "Listen to this evaluation of you from your boarding school. 'If you tell her to walk, she'll run. If you tell her to run, she'll walk. If you ask her to whistle, she'll sing; to sing, she'll whistle. She delights in stirring up the student body against any/all authority, and at best, her personality might be described as

147

refractory.' " The dean put down my file and said, "You didn't come highly recommended."

"Refractory?" I said.

"Hard to manage," she said.

"How come I got in here?"

"Part of it was my curiosity. Part of it was my interest in psychology. I teach psychology. Some of it was your stated interest in being a writer. I wanted to be a writer once, myself."

"My first choice was the University of Missouri, for journalism," I said.

"You could still make it," she said. "And meanwhile, we're very interested in starting a school newspaper. How would you like to work on the project?"

I knew I was going to like Vermont Junior College. That very first day, down in the basement "smoker," I puffed on cigarettes with my new classmates and heard an old, familiar song:

We are the girls from V. J. C., you see,
There's not a man in this damn nunnery,
And every night at eight they lock the door . . .

et cetera, et cetera.

That was the first time I heard about Justine Matso, too.

"Wait until you see her!" a senior said. "Of all the new girls, she's the beauty!"

"She looks enough like Lizabeth Scott to be her sister," another said. "She knows she looks like her, so she's copied everything about her—her hair, her walk, even her voice."

Lizabeth Scott was a new actress, a combination Lauren Bacall and Veronica Lake.

She was probably my favorite new movie star, but I didn't rush to get a glimpse of Justine Matso, who roomed in a different building than I did.

I was too overwhelmed by the idea there were boys on campus (local ones, about a dozen, who were day students) and too amazed that I could wear jeans to class, and to the dining room, and that I could carry a pack of cigarettes in my shirt pocket, though I could smoke them only in the "smoker."

I felt like someone who'd been let out of prison. I was finally going to school again with Yankees who talked like me, knew what deep snow was, and owned skis, skates, and toboggans. (Winters you could take skiing for gym, go off on skis before breakfast with the class, and come in to a feast of pancakes with real Vermont maple syrup poured over them.)

I was too busy clearing out an old storage room the dean allowed me to convert into a press room.

Before the autumn leaves had stopped falling, my first article appeared in the first issue of the school paper.

It was called "The Air and I," and it was about my flying lessons, which I'd talked my father into giving me that past summer. (My father'd bought a small plane for my older brother and him to enjoy, and I suppose I was in another phase of "brother envy.")

I hated flying, managed to solo, then never went up again.

. . . Now when people ask me why I never fly anymore, and add that aviation has a future, I agree that aviation has a

future, and I tell them I don't fly anymore because I want one, too.

So ended my first "published" article, never mind that *I* was the one who decided it should be published. . . . I was the editor of the paper.

Vermont Junior College, I began to see, was a place where I could begin to fulfill all my ambitions.

With boys on campus, I no longer got recruited for the male roles when I went out for drama. Excitedly, I wrote my mother that I had a lead role in the play *Berkeley Square.* No, I was not to be Tom Pettigrew or Mr. Throstle—I was to be the Lady Anne Pettigrew.

I was to star in that production with a new boyfriend— Bill Kerin, from Montpelier, Vermont, dark haired and blue eyed, a definite "catch" on a campus where girls outnumbered boys about ten to one.

It was then that Justine Matso first came to my full attention.

Justine was part of the Property Crew for that production.

She was also, I thought, slinking by Bill Kerin during rehearsals, smelling of Chanel No. 5, and brushing back that lock of long blond hair that hung provocatively down past her forehead, Lizabeth Scott style.

Shy, and not gregarious, Justine chose to room by herself in Old Main, and it was rumored that there were pictures of Lizabeth Scott everywhere on her walls and bureau top.

One evening some of my friends from the "smoker" and I wandered over to Old Main, where she lived, to see for ourselves.

Justine looked flustered and embarrassed when we dropped by her room. When we asked her why she had so many pictures of Lizabeth Scott around, she just shrugged and murmured, "Why shouldn't I?"

"Well, why shouldn't she?" someone said after we left there. "If *I* looked like Lizabeth Scott, I'd put up her pictures and copy her, too."

Then on a particularly cold winter afternoon (winter, there in Vermont, began in November), when it started to snow during play rehearsal, Justine hugged herself and shivered, and said she'd forgotten to bring her coat.

My Bill said she could wear his parka back to Old Main, and she did, while he trotted alongside her in just a sweater and I went my way in my warm pea coat.

"I was just being a gentleman," Bill told me that night during our usual phone conversation. "She's a nice girl. It didn't mean anything."

"Just because she looks like Lizabeth Scott, you drop everything and troop through a snowstorm for her without your coat!" I was angry.

"Why shouldn't she look like Lizabeth Scott? Lizabeth Scott is her sister."

"Oh, sure," I said, "and my sister's Bette Davis."

"She *is* her sister. She told me."

"And you believe her?"

"Justine's not the type to lie."

"Please!" I groaned. "Please spare me any more analyses of Justine Matso's character. It's not her character you're interested in."

"She doesn't want it blabbed all over, either," he said.

"I'm sure she doesn't," I said. "She's lying through her teeth!"

When I went down to the "smoker" for my last cigarette of the day, I told everyone what Bill had told me.

"She's after him," someone said.

"How's it going to help her to say Lizabeth Scott is her sister?" Kathy Mott wanted to know. "The way she looks, it wouldn't matter one way or the other." Kathy was always swooning over Justine's looks and complaining about her own stocky figure and frizzy blond hair.

Someone else said, "Justine's making herself important. It's not enough to *look* like a movie star, she has to say she's related to her, too!"

The next day some of us asked Justine outright if Lizabeth Scott was her sister.

"Yes," she said.

"How come you never told us?"

"I knew something like this would happen if I did."

"Something like what would happen?"

"I knew no one would believe me."

"Well, I *don't* believe you!" I said.

"I knew you wouldn't." Justine shrugged.

"How come all the photographs you have up are studio photographs?" someone said. "Anyone could write away and get those."

"I have other photographs," Justine said.

"Let's see them."

"I don't have to show them to you. I'm not under investigation."

"Does she write you?" we asked.

"Of course she writes me . . . when she gets time."

"Let's see one of her letters."

"Look," she said, "I don't have to prove anything to anyone. I'm not here as her sister. I'm here as Justine Matso."

"And her real name is Matso, too?"

Justine heaved a heavy sigh. "Yes, yes, yes, yes."

"It's just that you could settle everything for once and for all," I said, "if you could just prove it to us."

"I'm not interested in proving it to anyone," she said.

We went back to our building and down to the "smoker," where we wrote a letter to Lizabeth Scott, at Warner Brothers studio. We told her there was a student at V. J. C. posing as her sister. We signed it "The Curious Seven," c/o Kathy Mott.

Kathy made us all promise we'd apologize on our knees, in front of Justine, when Lizabeth Scott "verified" Justine's claim.

"She won't verify anything," I said. "We won't even get an answer. You have to be a cripple or something to get a personal reply from a movie star."

"Just lay off her until we get some verification," said Kathy. "You're using my name, and that's all I ask."

"Then we'll lay off her forever," I said, "because Lizabeth Scott isn't going to write to us."

One day the dean took me aside. "Why do you all care so

much about whether or not Justine is Lizabeth Scott's sister?" she asked me.

"Because she bragged about it to Bill Kerin."

"She didn't brag about it. Bill told me she just mentioned it, in a weak moment."

"Oh," I said, "great! A weak moment."

"Maybe it was his blue eyes." The dean chuckled.

"Not funny," I said. . . . "You know whether or not that's her sister. You have her file."

"Would you like me to share *your* file with everyone?"

"You win," I said.

———

Berkeley Square was a success, and Bill Kerin hadn't switched his attention from me to Justine, as winter really moved in.

Justine was dating a tall, handsome officer from Norwich University (New England's West Point), and whether or not she was Lizabeth Scott's sister didn't seem to matter as much anymore.

I insisted on taking Bill Kerin home with me for Christmas— *marring the postwar family celebration with a stranger* [my father wrote in his journal], *but she was determined to show him off to her friends. If he has anything going for him besides his looks, I'm in the dark about it. The silent type. Speaks only when spoken to. Twiddles his thumbs on the couch mostly.*

Bill was definitely not the silent type, anywhere but at my house. He just wasn't used to being called only by his last name, questioned in growls about his future plans, and looked in on, several times during the early morning hours, to be sure he was in the guest room and not in my room across the hall.

Bill nicknamed my father "Attila the Hun" and did imitations of him all the way back to V. J. C. on the bus: "What are you going to *be*, Kerin?" . . . "Kerin, what's your grade average?" . . . "What's a young man like you doing in a *junior* college, Kerin? That's all right for girls, but why are you going there, Kerin? Couldn't you get in anyplace else, Kerin?"

One of our "smoker" crowd was expelled for drinking shortly after Christmas, when the dean caught her staggering in from a date with a Norwich boy. This became our "cause" for a while, as we tried to reason with the dean, and the faculty, to get her back in school.

Drinking was the big taboo in that Methodist junior college. Norwich boys were known for their flasks filled with fruit juice and vodka, and their sweet tones telling girls in the backseats of cars: "If you don't like it, I'll stop I promise. But just see if you like it. I won't even touch your skin. Have some punch—there's nothing in this but juice."

We said that Norwich boys told three lies on the first date:

1. I'll stop.
2. I won't even touch your skin.
3. There's nothing in this but juice.

Our friend was forever lost to us, no matter our appeals and my editorial in the school paper entitled "To Err Is Human, To Forgive Divine."

That was the winter I fell under the spell of a new writer called Carson McCullers. That March I read and reread *The Member of the Wedding*, finding some of my old self in Frankie, the heroine, who changed her name to F. Jasmine Addams, "who belonged to no club and was a member of nothing in the world."

She gave herself a crew cut, age twelve years old, and was put out of her brother's wedding when she tried to go along with him and his bride.

But more than I could see a "yesterday me" in Frankie, I could see a future me in Carson McCullers. She became the one I most wanted to write like, and all my stories began to describe "a green and crazy summer," or "a green queer dream," or "a crazy queer green time," on and on.

Under the spell of McCullers, I sat in the pressroom typing out a story called "The Sister of Someone Famous," about a young girl who claimed a famous movie star was her sister.

She came out of the movie and the night outside was queer, with a hot wind and green-and-white moths nervous at window screens. When she thought what it would be like to have a star for a sister, stealing jealousy sickened her heart. . . .

The truth about Justine Matso no longer mattered to me. While Justine starred in the school's production of *Riders to the Sea*, I turned her into the sad heroine of a new short story, which I thought was the best I'd ever written. It probably was, with all its melancholy and many identical phrases lifted straight out of *The Member of the Wedding*.

Eric Ranthram McKay was dead, and Slater Burr was born, a new identity to author a series of McCullers-like tales about misfits and crazies in steamy little towns with names like Bulletsville.

I sent them out and they came back, sent them out and they came back, but "The Sister of Someone Famous" often received kind words written to Slater Burr across the form rejection slips by anonymous editors.

I never showed Justine Matso the story, but I showed it to others and it revitalized the notion that "poor Justine" was a fraud, albeit a very sympathetic one in my short story.

Lizabeth Scott was being heralded as the newest Hollywood siren. She was playing in a current movie called *The Strange Love of Martha Ivers*, with another new star called Kirk Douglas, and with Barbara Stanwyck and Van Heflin. Whenever we were wandering around Montpelier, we'd look through the movie magazines at the newsstand for stories about her. We figured she probably didn't even read her own mail . . . and if she did could care less about The Curious Seven, or the little girl in a junior college in Vermont who said she was her sister. . . . There were often stories about Lizabeth Scott, and pictures of her . . . never a mention of a sister, or that her real name was Matso.

I had other fish to fry. In addition to trying to launch Slater Burr's career, I was trying to get Marijane Meaker into the University of Missouri.

Along with the usual application blank, I sent clippings of my articles from the school paper. Thanks to an A+ in journalism, and one in English, I'd made the Dean's List . . . and the dean herself wrote a glowing letter of recommendation.

One afternoon in May, while Slater Burr was busy in the pressroom working on another story as Edith Piaf sang *"La Vie en Rose"* over the radio, one of The Curious Seven arrived with a letter.

> *Kathy Mott and The Curious Seven*
> *Vermont Junior College*
> *Montpelier, Vermont*

> *Dear Girls,*
> *I hope that my sister, Justine Matso, has made more trusting friends at that school than all of you. Since she hasn't mentioned any of your names in her letters, I assume she has.*
>
> *Sincerely,*
> *Lizabeth Scott*

That night, led by Kathy Mott, we trooped over to Justine Matso's room, showed her the letter, got down on our knees, and begged her forgiveness.

"Oh, get up!" she said. "Don't embarrass me!"

After the nervous laughter died down, we went red-faced back to the "smoker," to draw straws to see who would keep the letter with Lizabeth Scott's autograph.

About a week later, in the same mail with another rejection

slip for Slater Burr, I received word that I'd been accepted at the University of Missouri.

I never saw Justine Matso again after I left Vermont Junior College, but I saw every picture Lizabeth Scott made from *Dead Reckoning* with Humphrey Bogart to *Loving You* with Elvis Presley. Watching them, I always remembered that letter she wrote us, and I always saw Justine in her sister's sulky smile and sexy walk, and heard her in Lizabeth Scott's husky voice.

I'm sure that experience started me thinking about what it must be like to be related to someone famous. . . . Years and years later, I changed a word in the title of my old story "The Sister of Someone Famous," and wrote about *The Son of Someone Famous*. That story bore no real resemblance to my experience with Justine Matso, but it was set in a small town in Vermont very much like Montpelier.

Bill Kerin went into the Navy, and my father had to contend with another sailor in my life, that summer after I left Vermont.

I don't know whatever became of "my dean," Ruth Kingsley, though we corresponded for a while after I went to Missouri. But her decision to take a chance on me turned me around.

I can still remember my mother's voice over the telephone, when I called from school to tell her I'd made the Dean's List.

"Are you sure someone isn't playing a joke on you?"

Nine:
Rush Week

"I don't think you know what you're getting into," my father said. "There isn't any housing left at the university for out-of-state students. That means if you don't get asked to join a sorority, you have to come home."

He said that to me over and over that summer, but I don't think I understood what he was saying. I think if I'd really understood, I would have been too terrified to go through Rush Week at the University of Missouri.

Several times during the summer, strange, well-dressed, stiffly cordial women appeared at our house to look me over. These women were alumnae of sororities that had chapters at Missouri. They were women who lived in the east, in nearby cities, who'd been contacted by their former sororities and told to write up reports on me. It was their duty to evaluate me (and my family) to help the Missouri chapters decide whether or not I'd make a good Pi Phi, Tri Delt, Kappa, et cetera.

They didn't even scare me, because I didn't know enough about sororities to know that one bad word from them could kill my chances of getting into the sororities they represented.

I suppose a little of what could happen to me began to sink in when my father refused to ship my trunk on to Missouri until after Rush Week.

"If you don't make a sorority," he said, "you'll only have to ship it right back, so we'll wait and see."

Rush Week began a week before school began; so a week before the school year would be underway, I took a train to St. Louis, and then a bus to Columbia, Missouri.

On the bus I began to wonder what I'd done to myself.

In front of me, and behind me, Missouri girls who knew each other were riding in twos, talking excitedly about the Gamma Phis, the Thetas, the Pi Phis—"Greek" talk, and very Greek to me.

I didn't know anyone, and as I sat by myself on the long two-hour bus trip, I stared out the window at mile after mile of flat, barren land. No green hills or blue lakes—just flat earth and dust, and a creeping sense I was an outsider, as I heard the hum of conversation around me, and the laughter.

All rushees were put on several floors of a hotel in Columbia, five or six to a room.

It wasn't until I found my room that I also found a friend.

"Are you really from New York?" she said. "That's where I intend to live after 'J School'! My name's Ethel O. Orr, but call me E.O."

She was thin and pretty with red hair and freckles.

"I'm not from New York *City*," I said. "I'm from upstate."

"It doesn't matter," she said, "you're not from around here. I can't wait to get east and out of here! I want to be a Kappa." Then she sang this little song, some of which went "Ka-ap-pa, Ka-ap-pa, Ka-ap-pa Ga-am-ah, I am so god-damn glad that I am-am-ah Ka-ap-pa, Ka-ap-pa, Ka-ap-pa Ga-am-ah . . ." and she asked me what I wanted to be.

"Anything," I said.

"Anything?"

"If I don't make a sorority, I have to go home," and I explained to her about there not being any rooms left anywhere for out of staters.

"The war changed everything," she said. "There are students living in Quonset huts. But *don't* let anyone know you'll settle for anything. You have to play hard to get. I'm a Zeta legacy, but I'm not letting anyone know."

"What's a legacy?"

"A legacy is someone a sorority *has* to take. If your sister or your mother was in a sorority, then you're a legacy, and they have to take you!"

Then she explained that her sister had been a Zeta at another college, but she didn't want to be a Zeta.

"I want to be the best!" she said. "That's Kappa . . . or Pi Phi . . . but I want to be a Kappa."

Then she began to tell me about what sororities looked for,

about her theory concerning "sorority material."

"You're sorority material right away if your family's rich and well connected in the St. Louis-Kansas City area. It's going to be hard for you, coming from upstate New York."

"Why?"

"They look for girls who'll do them some good in St. Louis or Kansas City. If you're from money in St. Louis, for example, chances are you'll be a life-long contributor to the local chapter. You see what I mean?"

I saw. I was beginning to get depressed.

"But never mind," she said, "there are other things they look for, too. We'll talk about it, but let's go out and get a Coke and see if there're any cute guys around. Rushees get locked in at night, you know, and tomorrow we'll be going to all the rush parties."

We finished unpacking the clothes we'd brought for Rush Week, and took a walk through downtown Columbia.

E.O. told me she was eighteen, from Jefferson City, Missouri, and that all summer she'd dated a Sigma Alpha Epsilon who was in summer school at Mizzou. "That's what everyone calls Missouri—Mizzou—and SAE is a top fraternity. That's why I want to make Kappa. All the best frat guys date in Kappa, Pi Phi, and Theta. They're the big three."

There were signs in all the stores welcoming back the university students and the Stephens College girls.

"The Stephens girls are all high-hat," E.O. said. "They all have their noses in the air. It's like an eastern school. They don't have sororities."

We went into a soda shop (the Mizzou campus was off

limits during Rush Week), and E.O. said, "There'll be lots of Stephens girls in here. Mizzou girls stay around campus. So do the guys."

We ordered Coke, and E.O. told me she had her own Chrysler convertible. "It's only two years old and it's white, and it's one of the reasons I'll be sorority material. I hope! You can't drive a car during Rush Week, but I've got pictures of me in it, and I'm going to whip it out and show it around tomorrow during the rush parties. . . . Do you have a car?"

"I have one," I said, "but my family won't let me have it here."

"Too bad," she said. "That would help a lot. How are your grades?"

I told her my boarding-school ones were horrible, but I'd made Dean's List my freshman year at college. When I told her it was a junior college in Vermont, she made a face.

"Oh gawd," I said. "I guess I'm not sorority material."

"You could make a sorority, *probably*," she added ominously, "but it's hard to make the big three."

"I'll settle for anything," I said.

"Don't *say* that," she said. "Don't let anyone know you're desperate."

"You're not in my situation," I reminded her. "If you don't make one, you can live in a dorm and be an independent."

"I'd go home myself before I'd be an independent," she said. "If I don't make big three, I'll go home."

"I don't know what I've gotten myself into," I said.

"The trick is to make them think *you're* looking *them* over, not the other way around," E.O. said. "Be a little ritzy. Smoke foreign cigarettes. Talk up your boarding-school days. Forget the junior college. And don't latch onto markdowns!"

"What's a markdown?"

"You know how stores mark down things they can't get rid of? Markdowns are the ones no one talks to, or walks with from house to house. They're the losers and the duds. Don't feel sorry for them, and don't hang out with one of them. Remember: What you do this week will affect you the rest of the time you're at Missouri. You can't afford to be friendly with blackball material. You're better off staying on your own, even if it means walking through that front door all by your lonesome!"

I remembered E.O. saying that the next morning, when the taxis took our group to the very first sorority house: Kappa Kappa Gamma. E.O. and I went there in the same taxi, but as the six of us piled out, E.O. started up the walk without me.

"E.O.! Wait!" I called after her, but she didn't look back. Inside, E.O. was no friendlier. I was on my own

Being rushed was a lot like being back in Laura Bryan's ballroom dancing class, with other girls looking you over instead of boys.

There was even dancing, at ten in the morning, to records of Frank Sinatra and Harry James and Stan Kenton.

Kappas knelt at our feet, while we sat in chairs and let them light our cigarettes, and answered their questions.

Always, "Where are you from?" was first, and always, after I answered, I sensed a restlessness in the interviewer, and both of us began struggling to make conversation, before she was relieved by another Kappa. . . . Some of us seemed to be passed from Kappa to Kappa, while others were focused on by one girl, who danced with them and extended an invitation to "see the rest of the house."

I wasn't asked to dance or to see the rest of the house.

Across the room, E.O. was wowing them with photographs of her white Chrysler convertible.

"Gwendolyn," she called it. "I *have* to show you a picture of Gwendolyn!" I noticed she was smoking Players cigarettes through a long ivory holder, and blowing smoke rings . . . never once acknowledging me or looking my way.

All morning and afternoon we trooped from house to house through Greek Town.

Greek Town was just a few blocks, but it seemed like a little kingdom of luxurious houses, brick ones, southern-style ones with white columns, Spanish-style stucco ones, and old Tudor ones, all with bright-green manicured lawns, all displaying members' long, sleek cars in driveways and along the curbs out front.

Near the end of a long day, at the Alpha Delta Pi house, a short, thin brown-haired girl from Tulsa, Oklahoma, was particularly welcoming—"It's hard being from out of state, isn't it?"—and asked me if I wanted to see the rest of the house.

In the ADPi living room, E.O. finally made her way across to me, complaining of tired feet. We were all wearing spike heels.

"I can't wait to leave this dump and get back to the hotel," she whispered to me behind her hand. "How did you do to-day?"

"Okay."

"What do you mean? Did you get invited back?"

"Was I supposed to?"

"If they really, really want you, they usually say you're invited back."

"No one invited me back," I said. "Does that mean it's all over?"

"No. It just means no one's really hot for you. We'll nearly all get invited back to some houses. We'll find out which ones tonight."

"Did you get invited back?"

"Not by Kappa," E.O. said. "They adored me all over the Markdown Hotel Chain, but Kappa always plays it cool. I think."

"So did you play it cool at Kappa," I said. "You acted like you didn't know me. And not just at Kappa."

"Oh, honey," E.O. fibbed, "I was so nervous I didn't know what I was doing."

As we were leaving ADPi, Tulsa touched my sleeve and beckoned me from the line. 'We hope you'll come back tomorrow," she said.

I told E.O. about it in the taxi. "They hope anyone and everyone will come back," she said. "Not only are they part of the Markdown Hotel Chain, they also have an enormous quota to fill this year."

"What does that mean?"

"A lot of their seniors graduated last year, so now they've got to have a big pledge class to make up for it. If they don't keep the house filled, they don't meet their bills. So they're desperate."

"Sounds like we're made for each other," I said.

That night we all sat soaking our feet and waiting for the invitations to the next day's parties.

Everyone had become a little friendlier, and I began to meet some of the other rushees.

One, named Helen, was from Jefferson City.

"You must know E.O., then," I said.

"Ethel Orr?"

"Yes."

"Everyone knows Ethel Orr," she said coldly, and without any more explanation.

We were all gathered in a large lounge area that wasn't air-conditioned. We were sitting around in our slips and nighties, fanning ourselves and swallowing Cokes, looking at our watches anxiously. The invitations were supposed to be in by nine.

E.O. poked me in the ribs and gave me a crooked smile. "It's probably taking so long because your dear friends the ADPis are writing out so many invitations," she teased.

"Maybe it's taking so long because the Kappas are trying to remember your name."

"Just so long as they do," she said.

The Kappas, it turned out, didn't remember either of our names.

E.O. was amazingly philosophical about it, I thought. "I'll

just go with Theta," she said. "They're the only one of the big three who asked me."

Theta hadn't asked me.

"Go with Gamma Phi," E.O. advised as she flipped through my invitations. "And then Tri Delt, and Chi Omega; the others are on the M. H. Chain." I had six invitations back and E.O. had eight. We both had ADPi. So did a lot of girls.

"There's a girl here named Helen from Jeff City," I told E.O. "Do you know her?"

"We all know each other. What did she have to say about me?"

"Nothing. Just that she knew you."

"They're all jealous of Gwendolyn. I think those bitches at Kappa were, too."

After the invitations were delivered, some girls who didn't get any sat in tears; others went to their rooms, unable to face the rest. There were also girls weeping who hadn't gotten asked back to houses they'd aimed for.

"It'd be a lot worse if it weren't for the ADPis," E.O. said. "One girl only got one invitation. It was from them."

"I don't know how I got six," I said.

"You're an unknown quantity," E.O. said. "Coming from so far away, you're hard to really track down. That's for you and against you, at this stage."

E.O. and I stayed up in the lounge talking for a long time.

"Tomorrow night's going to be the killer," she said. "Even some of the ones who got six and seven invitations back aren't going to make it."

"Why would the sororities ask girls back if they're not interested?"

"To make it a good party, dummy," said E.O. "A big party is more impressive than a little one, so most of the houses ask back lots more than they'd ever pledge. . . . I heard the Kappas are only pledging three girls, and they've asked back about thirty. . . . I *know* why I didn't get asked back."

"Why?"

"I was at some SAE parties this summer, and I was popular. A lot of the boys liked me. It's jealousy. . . . Anyway, I'll be happy being a Theta. . . . If I pledge Theta, I'll have you over, as long as you promise not to have me over if you pledge ADPi."

Before we went back to our rooms to try and sleep, E.O. told me a story that kept me awake the rest of the night.

It was about a pledge who'd gone through Rush Week the year before.

E.O. named one of the big three sororities as the one whose alumnae promised them a new set of silverware, with their sorority crest on it, if they'd pledge this markdown named Marabelle.

"Now, Marabelle," said E.O., "was the creme de la markdowns. She was none too bright, acned, and bespectacled, shy and unskilled. She couldn't add up a column of figures, or run a hockey puck down the field, or sing a note, or say anything clever. She could afford a car, but she was afraid to drive. She could afford the best clothes, but she had no style. She didn't have anything going for her but the fact her family was teddibly well connected in St. Louis. Filthy rich, better family bit, and all—but she was the apple who *didn't* fall far from the family tree."

I liked listening to E.O. and already imagined us meeting for hilarious lunches in New York City, years after we were out of college. E.O. was going to be a newspaperwoman, she said, a gossip columnist. "I'll write novels on the side," she said. "It'll be my little hobby."

"Well," E.O. continued, "this sorority would have black-balled her in a second. No sorority would have asked her back, not even if she'd forgotten her purse. But after a lot of meetings, and a lot of pressure from the alum association, these darling girls decided to take her, to get the silverware, and to keep on the good side of the alums.

"So all through Rush Week they called her 'Silverware,' in their dark little meetings, after they agreed to take her."

"Did she ever find out?" I asked.

"Let me finish. Of course she found out. One of the actives had a little too much to drink one night and very kindly told her. Poor little Silverware took pills, almost kicked the bucket, too. Her family had to come in their big, long limousine and take her home."

"Thanks for the bedtime story," I said.

The next morning we went back to the sorority houses, and those of us with more than three invitations continued visiting the sororities through the afternoon. There was more dancing; there were skits performed; tea and punch were served in crystal glasses; there were iced centerpieces shaped like swans and ships, and fingerbowls with gardenias floating in them. One house had a piano player entertaining; another had a guitarist; at the Pi Phi there was a string quartet. E.O. made a joke that a girl played a comb in one house on the M. H. Chain.

There were themes to the parties: a rodeo party, a lawn party with the sisters in long gowns, a zodiac party, a pirate party, on and on.

At three houses I was taken aside and asked if I wanted to pledge. Two of them were on the M. H. Chain: ADPi and another; the third was Gamma Phi. I told Tulsa, at ADPi, that I wanted to join them.

"Are you friends with Ethel Orr?" she said.

"I just met her, but we're friends."

"We figured that you just met her. We're a little concerned, still."

"About what?"

"She was on campus all summer. They nicknamed her Easy Ethel. I think every guy in SAE had her."

"E.O.?" I said.

"E.O. She's got a bad rep. Her sister was the same way at S.M.U. The Zetas there kicked her out for being a nympho. They're two of a kind. Nouveaux riches from the war. They have everything but good taste."

"But you asked her back?"

"We ask a lot of people back we'd never pledge."

"And if I pledge, am I supposed to stop being friends with her?"

"We don't insist on that, but we hope you'll make new friends."

When I got back to the hotel, E.O. asked me if a sorority

had asked me "outright" to join. I told her I'd decided to be an ADPi. E.O. groaned and said I should have gone with Gamma Phi. "At least they're tonier."

Then she said no one had asked her outright. "But you never know anything for sure, until the bids come in tonight. Sororities have been known not to make a bid on girls they've asked, and to make one on girls they haven't asked. . . . But I'm sweating it. The Thetas didn't exactly fall all over me."

At ten o'clock that night the sorority bids were delivered to the hotel.

There was the ADPi bid, and five others, none from the big three.

E.O. refused to open any of her four bids; she knew from the envelopes which sororities had asked her to join. All were in the M. H. Chain.

"What are you going to do?" I said.

"I'm going to get Gwendolyn out of the parking lot and take off," she said.

"Some girls didn't get *any* bids," I said. You could hear the sobs of the ones who hadn't been asked to join a sorority. You could look around you and see their friends trying to comfort them. You could also see the friendless ones sitting sadly on their beds shamefaced, left out of the excitement as others whooped and danced around, waving their bids above their heads.

"Some girls didn't get any, right you are," E.O. said, "but I'd rather go home than belong to a club of leftover people."

"Hey!" I said. "That line's from Carson McCullers—a club of leftover people—that's from—"

"*The Member of the Wedding,*" E.O. said.

"I loved that book!"

"Then you should know how I feel," said E.O. "I loathe being unappreciated. And pull-leeze, no dramatics, my dear. It's been nice knowing you."

Then E.O. Orr began to pack, while I went downstairs to the lobby, to call my family collect, and tell them to send on the trunk.

Although E.O. and I promised to write to each other, we never did.

The sorority system, to my mind, is still one of the cruelest introductions to college life that I can imagine, and I'm not particularly proud of my participation in sorority life, even though I made my closest friends in the Alpha Delta Pi sorority.

I once wrote a book about Silverware, and about E.O. and some other experiences I'd had as a sorority girl, but it didn't translate "funny." It was an M. E. Kerr reject, a book that both my agent and Harper & Row didn't think was even worth rewriting.

Before it was rejected, I'd worked hard to come up with a good title for it. I tried to think what it was sororities were saying to their members, and it seemed to me they were all saying not to be individuals, but to be as much like the group as possible.

I called the book *I'll Love You When You're More Like Me.*

I finally used the title for another book, starring the son of an undertaker and the teenage heroine of a soap opera.

In this book the character named Sabra, who played a murderer's daughter on the TV soap, had this to say to her TV shrink:

SABRA: I didn't make Tri Ep.

DR. DAY: Do you blame your mother?

SABRA: Not really. I knew they wouldn't pledge me, even
           if Mom wasn't up on a murder rap. I'm not like them.

DR. DAY: Is that the only reason you think they don't want
           you?

SABRA: Isn't that always the only reason people don't want
           you? It's why they don't love you, too. All the cliques
           in the world from sororities to kaffeeklatches to your
           own relatives are saying just one thing to you: I'll
           love you when you're more like me.

Ten:
Sorority Life

We were always singing about things we'd get kicked out for doing.

We'd sit at the dining room table between courses, while uniformed blacks cleared the table, singing songs like:

My girl's an ADPi, she likes to drink my rye,
And she unties my tie, I'll never tell you why. . . .

or

Around the block she pushed a baby carriage,
She pushed it in the springtime and in the month of May,
And if you asked her why the hell she pushed it,
She pushed it for a Sigma Chi who's far, far away.

Behind the door her father kept a shotgun,
He kept it in the springtime, and in the month of May,
And if you asked him why the hell he kept it,
He kept it for a Sigma Chi who's far, far away.

Most of the songs were about drinking:

Drunk last night, drunk the night before,
Gonna get drunk tonight like I never got drunk before. . . .

and a lot were about sex:

As a silver dollar goes from hand to hand,
So a woman goes from man to man. . . .

There was rule after rule thwarting both activities, but that's what we sang about, with our plump, white-haired, southern housemother beaming at us from the head of the table.

Blind Date Week the pledges got their first taste of weekend sorority life.

The sorority Social Director fixed up each one of us with a blind date from the fraternity pledge lists.

We pledges wore little blue-and-white ribbons where our pins would be when we were finally initiated. We ranged in age from seventeen to nineteen, the majority from small towns in Missouri like Paris, Bolivar, and Poplar Bluff. The majority had never drunk before, were beginning smokers, and hadn't dated a lot; all were virgins.

The Social Directors of the sororities and fraternities tried their best to match lookers with lookers, losers with losers, in-betweens with in-betweens. There were long telephone calls from the ADPi house to the fraternity houses, as the matchmakers went down their lists of new pledges.

My first blind date was with an ATO.

He was a freshman from Centralia, Missouri, too young to have been in World War II, a thin, gangling fellow who wanted to be a newspaperman.

We walked in a group of six to the ATO house a few doors down the street.

The ATO housemother greeted us just inside the door, and we went down to the cellar, where there were booths and tables, and everyone was singing:

We are the great big BOOM! hairy-chested men,
BOOM! hairy-chested men, BOOM! hairy-chested men,
We are the great big BOOM! hairy-chested men,
We are the ATOs!

All the girls wore dresses, hose, and heels; the boys wore suits and ties.

You could barely make out ATO pictures and trophies on shelves around the room in the dim lighting. At the head of the room there was a large, circular bar, with a pledge behind it, opening bottles of Coke and ginger ale.

Liquor was forbidden at fraternity parties—not even beer was served—but most of the brothers carried little flasks with whiskey. Rye and ginger ale was the favorite drink.

Dwayne was my blind date's name.

For a while we tried shouting out things about ourselves, above the singing. Dwayne liked to hunt and fish, and he liked sports. His father was a pharmacist. He was an only child. He didn't read much, "some Hemingway."

We got tired of shouting after a while, and we drank and sang, sang and drank.

Finally I asked where "the powder room" was, and another ADPi pledge said she'd go with me.

"Only one at a time," said Dwayne. "That's a fraternity rule."

"That's a strange rule," I said.

Dwayne just shrugged and smiled and said, well, that was the rule. Then he showed me where to go.

Inside, the room was feminine and attractive, with a small dressing table, a flowered couch and matching chair, a soft rug, and a separate pink-and-blue bathroom.

Right before you stepped into the bathroom, you saw a huge cardboard figure of a man dangling on the wall to the left. The cardboard man was naked, except for a flapping fig leaf, across which was written LIFT AND LOOK!

That was what I did.

Suddenly, a fierce sound rang out, a wailing bell that wouldn't stop.

Humiliated, I went into the bathroom while it persisted, and stayed until it stopped.

Then I dawdled before the mirror, trying to prepare myself for the embarrassment of facing everyone who knew by then I'd lifted the fig leaf.

I could hear the singing before I opened the door.

I came out to a long line of ATOs and their dates, chorusing:

Never lift a fig leaf, lady, just to steal a glance,
Unless,

Unless,
You fol-low with ro-mance!
Never lift a fig leaf, lady, let the poor guy be,
That is,
That is,
If it's idle cu-ri-os-i-ty!

Pushing her way past me, nearly knocking me over to get inside, was a very sick Chi Omega pledge who'd had too many rye and gingers.

My date, Dwayne, was in stitches.

"I knew you'd do that!" he guffawed.

"Someone's about to vomit in there," I said.

"That's Jim Butler's date. She only had three drinks."

I went back inside to see if she was okay. In between retching sounds she said to please leave her alone.

That wasn't the last time I heard those sounds that evening.

After we finally got back to the sorority house, in time for the one-o'clock curfew, there were the same sounds coming from the upstairs johns. If we had to wait several months to be initiated into the sorority, we didn't have to wait for our initiation into sorority life.

Some pledges got sick, some passed out. Most sat around on beds and floors in crowded rooms, doing up their hair, comparing notes: who got "stuck," whose date got "tight as a tick," whose was all hands, whose asked for another date, on and on.

Across the street at the Gamma Phi house, the Betas had arrived to serenade, and everyone rushed to the windows to watch them as they carried lighted candles and gathered on the Gamma Phi lawn:

Golden slumbers kiss your eyes,
Smiles awake you when you rise,
Sleep, pretty Gamma Phis, do not cry,
Betas sing a lullaby, lullaby, lullaby. . . .

"What's the rule about dating independents?" someone asked.

We were attending the weekly pledge meeting, led by the Pledge Director, who explained the rules, assigned the pledge lessons, and meted out the punishment for demerits. (One of the punishments was taking the housemother to a movie on a Sunday afternoon.)

My old friend, Tulsa, was that year's Pledge Director.

"Okay," she said, "that question always comes up among new pledges. We have no real rule about it. However, you joined a sorority because you found a gang you can really be proud of, right? Most men join fraternities for the same reason. They want to be with a gang they know has high standards and high ideals . . . right? . . . Now, to my way of thinking, it's only logical to want to date your match."

"But," the questioner persisted, "may we date an independent if we find that his standards are high and he has high ideals? I mean, all independents can't automatically have low standards and low ideals."

"We don't have a real rule about it, but we'd prefer that you date fraternity men on weekends."

"But," the questioner wouldn't stop, "a lot of really sharp

guys are independents. *Most* vets are; most guys going through school on the G.I. Bill are, and they're older, more interesting."

"Unless you've got a specific request about an independent, don't take up time in our meeting with this kind of talk," Tulsa said. "We don't have any prejudice against independents, but birds of a feather flock together, right? . . . Why else did you join a sorority?"

Then Tulsa assigned the pledge lesson (learn the first three songs in the Alpha Delta Pi songbook, and the names of the official alumnae officers) and dismissed the group.

Exiting, under her breath, one of the pledges sang a familiar song:

> *He's a goddamn independent,*
> *He's a G.D.I.*
> *Ignore! Ignore! Ignore the bas-tard!*
> *Ditch the guy,*
> *The G.D.I.*

"We ought to count our blessings," someone else said. "In some of the houses they *do* have a real rule about it. They . . . *don't* . . . date . . . them."

I was already writing tragic stories, exaggerating life on sorority row, never one to get an idea about the doughnut when the hole made more compelling fiction.

I wrote a story called "Frat Boy" about a weakling from a small town in Missouri, who pledged ATO and was made to strip to the waist "revealing his hairless, hollow chest" and to pound his chest and sing:

We are the great big BOOM! hairy-chested men

to the ridicule of his fraternity brothers and their dates.

That story was followed by "Pledge," about a girl in love with a poor boy from her small town—both at the same university—she a member of a sorority at her mother's insistence, and he the independent she couldn't date.

I made friends with Miggie, a girl in my writing class, who was an independent from St. Louis. We conferred with each other about where to send short stories. She told me the J School students who wanted to be writers had an old saying that you'd never commit suicide as long as you had a manuscript in the mail. The trick was to keep your stories circulating; always have at least one "out."

I did. I accumulated a stack of rejection slips.

Miggie got me interested in the life of F. Scott Fitzgerald, and whispered to me on the way to class one day, "Zelda, his wife, died in a fire, in an insane asylum."

I became enraptured with Fitzgerald, and wore out a copy of his autobiographical pieces called *The Crack-Up.*

I went through it circling words like "insouciance" to look up in the dictionary, and marked things like "Life burned high in them both." I passed Miggie notes in class telling her Fitzgerald was right when he wrote that all good writing was swimming underwater and holding your breath. She passed me poems she'd written with lines like

Blue lights in a black bottom
Here we go round

Blue lights in a black bottom
Phrase makers make no sound.

I met a boy named Dick Matheson who wrote weird fantasies I envied, because they were so good, and were always read aloud in writing class by Dr. Peden.

At a sorority masquerade I went as a rejection slip, wearing a full-length black slip with all my rejections from magazines, big national ones and little literary ones, pinned to it.

As usual, I spent a lot of time in the library.

I noticed a young man in charge of the reading room, my favorite place in the library. He was a sharp-featured, not-very-tall fellow, who always wore a dark turtleneck sweater and a light jacket. . . . He had a shy, crooked smile, a dimple, and he spoke with an accent.

I began watching him.

I found out his name was George.

I found out he was Hungarian, and overheard him explaining some of the "wisual aids" the library offered. His v's became w's.

I made up my mind to strike up a conversation with him the next time I went to the reading room.

I went there the day after I made up my mind, but he was gone.

They told me he'd quit, to take a part-time teaching job (Spanish) at Stephens College.

I'd begun keeping a journal à la Scott Fitzgerald, I fancied. I wrote in it, "Soon after I found George, I found him gone."

But George wasn't gone . . . not by a long shot.

The initiation into the Alpha Delta Pi sorority was fraught with capers that would have caused Ape, of Stuart Hall, to swoon from a surfeit of tawdriness.

Blindfolded, pledges were led into bathrooms and ordered to pick out whatever was floating in a toilet bowl and eat it (bananas). We were ordered to "lick ick" off sidewalks (raw eggs) and walk barefoot through rats' intestines (raw liver).

We had to wear dunce caps to class, some of us—others wore tight bathing caps on their heads with white paint on their faces, MORON across their foreheads in red lipstick.

We had to walk on all fours like dogs the length of beerhalls, where students hung out, barking for beer we were made to chugalug. Prone on sidewalks, in front of campus buildings, we had to "fry like eggs." We carried mops and pails to clean up gutters on main streets, and to return to the sorority house with no less than three hundred filthy cigarette butts picked off the pavement. We danced jigs on command, anywhere on campus, and kissed the shoes of our sorority sisters whenever we encountered them.

I had a reputation as the problem pledge. I missed too many meetings, and caused too much trouble during the ones I attended. ("Why do we have to swear we're members of the Caucasian race when we take the sorority oath of allegiance?" was one of my questions. "Why don't we ever have exchange dinners with Jewish fraternities?") There was a feeling I didn't have a proper reverence for sorority ritual, that I hung out too much with my friend Miggie, an independent, and that I made trouble purely for the pleasure of making trouble.

I was hazed with a vengeance. My final assignment was to find my way back from a country road, where I'd been left barefoot, after being driven there blindfolded.

Almost immediately I thumbed a ride with a farmer, and had him drop me off at Miggie's dorm.

I stayed there and let ADPi sweat, right up until late-night curfew.

Grease on my face, dirt on my clothes, torn blouse, limping, I made my entrance just as they were about to call the police and risk censure from The Panhellenic Association for "undue hazing harassment."

"Oh, thank God you're safe!" our housemother cried out. (We'd become fast friends, since I'd earned so many demerits I was always made to take her to the movies Sunday afternoons. I'd gone to more movies with Mother Nesselbush that fall than with any other person in my entire life.)

I made up a story about what had happened to me, how I'd escaped hoodlums, on and on. I doubt that anyone believed me.

Later, one of the pledges said, "We ought to count our blessings. At one of the houses they make you get in a coffin, and they nail down the top and just leave you there for a whole day!"

We were always coming up with reasons for counting our blessings, because it was worse somewhere else.

The next night, in a candlelit ceremony, with everyone in long white dresses, singing softly "I Will Be True, White and Blue" to "Mood Indigo," Tulsa pinned the diamond-shaped ADPi emblem above my heart.

As she kissed me in a sisterly gesture, she whispered into my ear, "I never thought you'd make it."

Then we were allowed to know what the secret sorority handshake was—one finger scratched the palm of the other person, a handshake that was known in upstate New York as a dirty one boys gave girls (whatever it was supposed to mean to the girls never quite clear).

. But that was our sorority handshake, and after the demonstration we went about nicking each other's palms with our long fingernails, singing "I Love to Wear the Diamond Pin."

February 1947, our sorority house was getting ready for a show called *The Spring Follies*, and I was working on lyrics to the song "Chicago."

Instead of

Chicago, Chicago—it's a hell of a town,

I'd begun a lyric

ADPi, ADPi—it's a hell of a house!

If I came up with a song the sorority could sing in the show, I'd be excused from song practice for the semester. This would benefit both the sorority (I was tone deaf) and me (more free time to write).

Because I couldn't remember how "Chicago" went, I took myself "uptown" to buy a Tommy Dorsey album featuring it.

I was waiting in line, holding the album, when a voice spoke up behind me. "How can you listen to such junk? 'Havaiian

Var Chant,' 'Chicago,' 'Boogie Voogie,' 'Somevhere a Woice is Calling.' "

I turned around and found George again, with his v's w's and his w's v's.

" 'Boogie *Voogie*'?" I said, " '*Havaiian Var* Chant'?"

"You're the girl from the library," he said. "I thought you had more brains, but look what you're buying!"

"What are you buying?" I said.

"I don't buy. I browse," he said, "but if I had money to buy, I vouldn't buy such junk."

"I'm buying it for the sorority," I said, "not for myself."

"I thought you had more brains than to be in a sorority."

I've never met anyone like him in my whole life [I wrote in my diary that night], *and I never will! He's originally from Budapest, from the Pest side, he said. "You can remember that because I will become a pest in your life and make you think about more important things than Tommy Dorsey and sororities." He's not like the other boys around here. In fact, he's a man, because he saw horrible things before he got out of Hungary. He wants me to join The Cosmopolitan Club. He wants me to meet him tomorrow. I love his accent and the way he walks with his hands behind his back and the scarf around his neck flung over his back. I told him I hate my name, Marijane, and he said what was my middle name? I told him it was worse—Agnes. He said in Hungarian Agnes was very pretty. It's Agi. He said if I wanted him to, he'd call me that. I want him to!*

That summer I stayed in summer school to be near George. All my letters home were about George.

Concerned, my mother sent me a *Reader's Digest* reprint of an article called "Does Your Daughter Think She's in Love?" Underlined was

Most men despise the girls who yield to them. . . . That's one reason why girls are to be pitied when they do yield. It isn't pleasant to be despised by the person you've sought to please.

My father took a different tack. He decided it was time for my mother and him to pay me a visit.

Christmas 1948, I read his summary of this visit.

Columbia is a western college town, overcrowded but without many places for entertainment. Mostly beer joints where students can spend an evening for a dollar.

Marijane is serious-minded, seriously interested in her college life and this writing ambition, and fortunate in her situation in the ADPi sorority, where she has the companionship of so many fine girls.

We met this George she thinks she's in love with. He is a smart, bright-looking young man, here in the U.S. by way of a concentration camp, Venezuela, and a Venezuelan scholarship. He is an intense, hard-working student teacher, but so thoroughly indoctrinated with Communist teaching that everything is wrong with every other way of living.

We think Marijane is levelheaded enough to handle this. We pray she is! At least he is better than the usual drinking and drivel-talking college-boy type.

That same summer my parents visited me, I joined the Communist Party—not another youth group as I had, for a lark, when I was in boarding school, but the real thing.

With George, and other party members, I journeyed to St. Louis to meet William Z. Foster, the head of the Communist Party. On the way, in the car, we all sang, "Arise, ye prisoners of starvation," and *"Bandiera Rosa—Triumfera!"*

Though we saw each other every day, and talked for hours, we wrote each other every day, too, letters of love for each other *and* the Party.

> *I am so happy to be with you, Agi, so depressed every time I have to leave you—so aware of the fact that you are the girl I was waiting for, and I feel blood circulating gaily and unselfconsciously in my veins, and you the life to my pulse. . . . Learn to observe dialectically, Agi, and do not protest so much against my love of the intimate and my aversion to the cheapened values. Man got his first chance in 1917, and he took it! Look at the Soviet youth—their confidence and strength and brotherly spirit! And know that the old, old words of love will never be used in vain toward you by your loving comrade, George.*

After one Party meeting, a comrade remarked on the book I was carrying: *Raintree County* by Ross Lockridge. My pal Miggie and I were raving to each other about Lockridge, speculating over coffee about how he could have killed himself, age thirty-three, just when his book was at the top of the best-seller list.

Miggie and I saw him as a new Thomas Wolfe.

"Why are you reading that book?" my comrade asked me. She was a political science major, a hefty girl from Kansas

City who often glared at my sorority pin in meetings and always called me Comrade Mary Ann, never getting my name right.

"He's a new Thomas Wolfe!" I exclaimed.

"Thomas Wolfe was a decadent writer," she said, "and so is this Lockridge. The capitalistic system killed this Lockridge. He had to pander to popular taste to make a buck."

"Who's a good author to read?" I asked.

"Karl Marx," she said. "Nikolai Lenin."

Around that time, my first poem was published in *The Midland Review.*

"We pay in prizes only, and we're unable to send out gratis copies," they advised me.

The poem was called "Boom! (for George)."

Its last seven lines read:

Take me from a crowd to a quiet room.
Kiss me—say nothing
Look at me only—and then
Forget with me, so that we may remember.
And never wonder—never doubt
Never believe anything except
That this is comme il faut.

Comme il faut? . . . This from someone who barely passed French II.

But I didn't know enough, yet, to be embarrassed by "Boom!"

I ran to George with a copy, and the news it was actually going to appear in print.

"It's a very sweet poem, Agi," he said, "and thank you. I'll write you one when I get time."

I didn't very much like the idea that he thought he could just sit down, when he got time, and scribble me a poem. . . . I liked it even less when he did.

He who had never once expressed any interest whatsoever in writing found time between teaching, studying, politicking, et cetera, et cetera, to scratch out a little thing for me, clearly superior to anything I could come up with.

"Dear," it was called.

Am I dear to you?
I wish I were—
Dear is held in mind in warm rooms of thought
Do I live there?

Do I sit at the fireplace of your eyes?

Dear you call me
I wish I knew—
Dear is the tear, the wind soft voiced, the peaceful word
Is there peace in you?
Is there quiet knowledge and knowing smile?

Dear walks with me
I wish it would stay
Dear is the shadow, reflection of us,
Ours in light, yet also in darkness
Are you going my way?
I wish you would.

"Dear" was testing me dearly.

I was supposed to be the writer.

It took just three blackballs to keep a girl from being asked to join a sorority.

Together with two sorority sisters I'd been working on, we blackballed every pledge who came through Rush Week, as a protest against the whole idea of the blackball system.

Blackballs were always given in secret. No one knew who made a blackball when the slips of paper were put into the hat.

"*What* is going on here?" the sorority president asked. "We can't admit any new pledges, since all of them get blackballed!"

"Why don't we just admit everyone?" I suggested.

"We don't have *room!*"

"Well"—I shrugged—"then we can't take any new members in, I guess."

"Are you behind this?"

"Blackballs are secret," I said.

"You're behind it, all right," she said. "Look! This is a *sorority*! This isn't a boarding house! We pick and choose!"

"It's a decadent system," I said.

"And you're a Red!" she screamed.

Sorority meetings became angry battlegrounds, infiltrated with the philosophy of one of its members working hard to "observe dialectically" and rid herself of "cheapened values."

"We don't insist that a sister's date wear evening clothes to a formal party," the Social Director told me. "We've been tolerant of men in suits and ties at formal affairs, and you know it. . . . But we *do* draw the line at turtleneck sweaters under sports coats."

"He doesn't own a shirt and tie," I said. "That's bourgeois."

"Then tell him we're bourgeois and we don't need him around with his long face and his snide remarks. He's such a party pooper, too!"

"I need him around!" I insisted.

But many nights, on weekends, George was waiting tables at local restaurants, and afterward too exhausted to go out.

I began dating Lester, an independent from Oak Park, Illinois, I'd met in English class. He was going for a Ph.D. He wanted to become a professor of English. He was tall and lean and towheaded. He was reading everything Sigmund Freud had written . . . and everything I had, too.

On May 3, 1948, Henry Wallace visited Columbia, Missouri, during his campaign for the United States presidency.

"I have a lot to do for the party," George told me, "so I'm not going to attend the rally with you. Go with your sorority sisters."

"Don't tell me who to go with. I thought I was going to be an usher."

"Just go with your sorority sisters!" he said. "Please! I have too much to think about. I can't worry about you."

The Communists were supporting Wallace.

I was probably the only sorority member present wearing a Wallace button.

There was a crowd of five thousand gathered before the

platform, on the Boone County courthouse lawn.

Even before Wallace began speaking, trouble was brewing.

When a female faculty member from Lincoln University (black student body) spoke, a chant began:

We don't want her
You can have her
She's too black for us! . . .

"Black," in those days, wasn't meant to describe a black; it was meant to ridicule one. . . . Missouri was still a very southern state, and the university did not accept black students.

Small flying objects began falling near the speaker's stand: clumps of grass, orange peels, paper wads, pebbles.

The black woman couldn't continue speaking. "Nigger!" was yelled at her.

There was pushing and shoving in the crowd, and banners were beginning to appear saying things like "Go Back to Russia!" and "Wallace Is a Commie!"

By the time Henry Wallace stood up to speak, the hecklers were in full force.

We don't want him
You can have him
He's too red for us!

The chant was a takeoff on a popular song:

I don't want him,
You can have him,
He's too fat for me. . . .

A chorus of boos welled up in the midst of Wallace's speech.

"What about Russia?" a heckler shouted. "It ain't no democracy!"

A tomato hit the black woman's legs as she sat behind the speaker's podium.

More flying objects.

The police began moving in, and students who had climbed trees were yelling, "Red! Red! Red!"

When it was finally all over, as we made our way back to the sorority house, some of my sisters were changing their tunes.

"I was ashamed," one said. "I never saw anything like that. That poor colored woman!"

"Wallace wasn't saying anything I don't believe in," another said.

"I might even vote for him, just in protest at what happened," a third.

Late that night, George called.

"Wasn't that terrible today?" I said.

"It was terribly successful," he said. "It was exactly what we wanted. Our chants got everyone going. Mob psychology, Agi—it never fails."

"*Our* chants?"

"Our chants, our rotten tomato—I got that one to splatter all over the place myself. Pretty good aim, hah? We started it and the bourgeoisie finished it! Wait until you see the newspapers tomorrow, Agi! Free speech was denied. A Negro woman was humiliated! What a disgrace to a big university! We'll get plenty of space, and plenty of sympathy! I'll meet you for a coffee to celebrate!"

George was right.

It made all the national papers, headlines in *The New York Times.*

The next day nearly every professor stopped his class long enough to express outrage at the students' behavior and bigotry.

"All you have to do in a southern crowd is toss out the word 'nigger' to get the hackles up!" George said.

"Somebody could have really gotten hurt," I said.

"That's exactly why I told you not to usher, and to go with your sorority sisters," George said.

"You protect your own," I said, "but what about others? What about 'the people'?"

"Don't pick, Agi, please. It was a great wictory!"

For the first time, the way he said his v's like w's wasn't all that endearing.

I was beginning to wonder about things like was it worth headlines to toss out the word "nigger" to get the hackles up, and to toss a rotten tomato at a black woman?

We began having our differences.

I began seeing more of Lester, who'd convinced me to switch my major from journalism to English literature. I wanted to write, and to get a job in publishing after graduation, not in advertising or on a newspaper. I wanted to take all the English courses I could, not courses called "The History of Journalism in the State of Missouri," or "Principles of Advertising."

Caught up in college life, and still in my infatuation with George, I had no interest in going home. (My kid brother was eight by then; my older brother was studying at Yale, married, and the father of twin boys.)

I decided to stay in school for another summer.

It was a summer that began with George and me sniping at each other.

I was caught up with the Republican and Democrat conventions, while George said none of it mattered because both Dewey and Truman were Wall Street puppets. . . . He was concerned with the new state of Israel and the resultant war in Palestine.

He was trying to get me to listen to the Rasoumovsky quartets by Beethoven. I wanted him to hear Duke Ellington's "Three-Cent Stomp" and the new bebop sound in Ella Fitzgerald's "Lady Be Good."

"All of that music exploits fine Negro talent!" he'd complain.

I was reading Yeats and Virginia Woolf and Proust and Gide, all of whom he deplored—"None of them gave a damn for the working man!"—and he was reading Howard Fast and Frederick Engels and heavily underlining for me passages in *What Is Philosophy?* by Howard Selsam, like

We are the victims of the economic machine under which we live, not its masters.

He was working very hard for the party, and to support himself in school. I had few classes, and a lot of free time. I volunteered to help out at nearby Fulton State Hospital, an institution that held 2500 mentally sick patients.

"We have only one registered nurse in the entire place," the doctor told us, as he led us on our initial guided tour, "and all the attendants are untrained. Only a hundred and forty-four patients are undergoing active treatment."

We were a half dozen student volunteers who were there to conduct classes in everything from finger painting and social dancing to creative writing.

I was in charge of the creative writing class. Eight patients were assigned to me.

We met in a room in the clinic, far away from locked wards we'd visited where patients were tied down, locked into narrow cells, or moping around open wards talking to themselves, not speaking at all, or being swatted with heavy wet towels when they "acted up."

Some in my class wrote gibberish, and some wrote touching memories of their life outside, and one man sat grinning, saying, "We're all nuts here, and anything we write will come out nuts!"

We met every Saturday afternoon, and often, after, we joined the dancing to records like Nat King Cole's "Nature Boy," Peggy Lee's "Golden Earrings," and Perry Como's "Haunted Heart."

The psychiatrist in charge was a native of India, educated at the University of Kansas, and trained at the Menninger Foundation in Topeka.

Gurbax Waraich was a tall, dark-haired, dark-eyed bachelor in his forties, and he began inviting me to have dinner with him in the staff dining room.

I began to think I'd rather be a psychiatrist than a writer.

I began to spend a lot of free time at Fulton, visiting wards with him, listening to him talk about patients, and trying to hide the fear and revulsion I felt at what I saw and heard and smelled.

There was no television yet to distract the patients, no tranquilizers, just scenes of inactivity, with most sick people sunken into deep depressions and dejection in their rocking chairs, deteriorated and hopeless. Some wore leather cuffs. Some curled up on the floor in pools of their own urine.

"Anyone who can sign his name can get a job here as an attendant," Gurbax told me. "There are no requirements at all for attendants who are given the custody of these people. And these people, more often than not, are physically sick as well as mentally sick."

"I think I want to be a doctor," I'd tell him when we'd talk.

"Wanting to help people isn't a good enough reason for becoming a doctor," he'd argue. "It's a long road, becoming a doctor. You have to be good at science and language. You can help people, in your chosen profession, by writing about them. You're good at that, so do what you're good at."

"I can't help people like this by writing."

"People like this, a lot of them, became this way because of neglect, and neglect keeps many of them this way. You can write about that. . . . For instance, some of the women here are here because they were brutalized by their fathers and brothers. You can write about that. No one writes about incest, or about what happens in homes of poorly educated, deprived people. They take it out on each other. The husbands take it out on the wives and the children; the wives take it out on the children; the older children victimize the younger children . . . and so on."

I would go back to school late Saturday nights, and meet George when he was finished working behind the counter of a campus cafeteria.

"Now you know what a capitalistic system does to people," he'd say. "Now you see for yourself!"

I'd tell Gurbax what George would tell me, and he'd say, "No system can teach people how to love and nurture. All systems have their flaws when it comes to that."

George would wave away any rebuttals.

George would say, "He's an Indian—they're all filled with lofty talk and mysticism, while their streets are filled with beggars and they persist with an unjust caste system!"

I began to date Gurbax. He'd drive from Fulton to Columbia, and I'd take him to the campus cafes filled with students and the smell of beer and the sound of the jukebox, and we'd sit shouting over the noise while I drank drafts and he sipped ginger ale.

"He's a dreamer!" George would attack him. "He's not a doer. I'm a doer!"

"Sometime," Gurbax would say, "I'd like to be psychoanalyzed. I've never had time for that. I've never gotten to know myself."

"Psychoanalysis," George would say, "is the invention of a bourgeois biologist who thought you could put people under microscopes like bugs! We have no time to look inward! We need to look out and around us, and see what's happening to victims of an unfair economic system!"

On and on, back and forth.

I didn't do much writing that summer. I wasn't sure, anymore, how I really felt about anything.

By late August the anti-Communist fervor was sweeping the country. The House of Representatives was investigating un-American activities. Whittaker Chambers, a senior editor of *Time* magazine, was accusing Alger Hiss, president of the Carnegie Endowment for International Peace, of having been a Communist when he worked for the State Department in the thirties.

Communist Party leaders were being arrested for advocating the overthrow of the government.

That pressure, and financial pressure, made George decide to ship out of the United States, to go to Caracas and visit his mother, before returning "permanently" to Hungary.

> *We're still on the Mississippi* [he wrote], *so I can't say I have left the States behind, even though for all practical purposes I have. How do I feel about leaving? No way. I have no overall attachment to this country, not because I'm not an American, but because my country is the movement, and my fellow citizens the workers everywhere.*
>
> *There are people, though, that I hate to leave. You are one of them, Agi, made of velvet and marble. We had a wonderful time together, didn't we? I have already placed you so close to me as very few persons*

*have ever been, and will be, so I cannot say good-
bye ever. Just love, your George.*

In 1949 I was graduated from the University of Missouri.
Together with two sorority sisters, I set off for New York
City, to find a job in publishing, until I could become published
myself and be a full-time free-lance writer.

For years I corresponded with George, who chided me from Hungary for things America was doing.

Talking about your news service and the like [a typical
letter would read], *we get a big kick out of the fantastic
stuff you daily tell about us. You're far from smart. What
the hell do you think those miners at Dorg thought when
one day they were notified by your Voice of America
that 80 of them were shot by Communist police? What
our workers always do in face of your provocations is
raise their production and enjoy life better in their new
modern apartment houses—one in every five days on
the average which we're building in this our first 5-year
plan.*

In another, he wrote:

*I work just in front of your embassy and day by day
see so-called diplomats with faces like Missouri baseball
players walk around our streets as if they were super-
men, on their favorite hobby—spying!*

Then, in 1953, there were no answers to my letters to George.
I did not hear from him again until February 1957.

My dear Agi,

*I know that if this letter ever reaches you, it'll be a
real miracle, as I only have your address of several years
ago, and you're not the type of person who wouldn't
move around a lot.*

*But I do feel the urge of letting you know that on
December 30 my family and I escaped from Hungary,
and are now awaiting transportation to Venezuela, where
my mother still lives.*

*Are you surprised, honey? My ideas have changed
during the last few years. I have been completely disillu-
sioned with that thing falsely called Socialism which I
found in Hungary, culminating in the brutal, beastly sup-
pression of the people's revolution in 1956.*

*I was fed up with the whole thing a long time ago,
but now I simply couldn't stand it any longer, and don't
want to see my children be brought up in that awful
setup.*

*Besides, I took part in the preparation for the revolu-
tion, and would have been arrested.*

*My wife and I crossed the frontier walking for four
hours in deep snow, across fields and woods, carrying
nothing else than our small children in arm. (Two daugh-
ters, Agi, one two years old and one just past six
months.)*

*We are living 20 miles from Vienna in a refugee home
maintained by the American Mennonites. They are pretty
nice people. We'll have to wait about three more weeks*

*before we'll be taken to Italy, and then to Venezuela
by boat. (But my letters will be forwarded from here.)*
   What are you doing?
   Where are you?
   Don't tell me you're married, too.
   *I thought of you a lot last week while reading an article
on Thomas Wolfe in an issue of* Life. *It was about his
correspondence concerning* Look Homeward, Angel. *I
know you loved Wolfe and his books.*
   *Have you any friends in Vienna? I would like to meet
them. Boy, it's a grand feeling to be able to meet people
and to write to people freely again!*
   *I hope you will answer me right away, dear Agi, if
you only get this.*
                               Love, George

The last time I saw George, we had dinner together in my
apartment in New York City, 1968.

After he told me all about his wife and children, he looked
across the table at me and said, "Eleven years ago I was afraid
I'd be pushed into a Soviet tank and deported to Russia, as so
many young Hungarians were. Now I sit here with you in this
Greenwich 'Willage' apartment, listening to your jazz music I used
to complain to you about. . . . Life is funny, isn't it, Agi?"

Eleven:
New York

"If you don't know shorthand," my father told me, "you won't be able to get a decent job anywhere."

I took a four-week business course, to learn shorthand, the summer before I joined my sorority sisters.

I could never master it. I drew shorthand instead of writing it.

About all I was fit to do in an office was file, answer the phone, and take interoffice mail from floor to floor.

I found a job in the production department at Dutton Publishing, at thirty-seven dollars a week.

I did menial work. At Christmas my boss, who was the art director and a conscientious teetotaler, sent me around the company with bottles of liquor he'd received as gifts from printers and artists, to sell for the highest price to other employees.

I loved the job, but I wasn't worth the thirty-seven dollars a week they paid me. I sat at a desk working on my own ideas, watching the production of book jackets for authors like Gore Vidal, Mickey Spillane, and Anaïs Nin, dreaming of the day I'd see my own name on the cover of a book.

I wrote to agents I hoped would read my stories and want to represent me.

I hung around with a crowd of would-be writers, many of them Missouri graduates, all of us comparing notes on how to go about getting our work published.

We all talked about Dick Matheson, the boy whose stories were always read aloud back in my writing class. He'd already sold some stories to science fiction magazines; he already had an agent.

"You can't get anywhere without an agent," one fellow insisted. "It's like a whore trying to get somewhere without a pimp!"

"If you send a story to a magazine, and you don't have an agent," someone else said, "you end up in the 'slush pile.' Most of the time no one even reads anything in the slush pile!"

My roommates had good jobs. One, trained in Journalism School, was hired by J. Walter Thompson, advertising. The other, who knew shorthand, became a secretary at Fawcett Publications. Both were making fifty dollars a week.

We eventually found two other roommates, and we all took

a large two-bedroom, two-bathroom apartment up in Washington Heights.

To get to Dutton Publishing Company every morning (in hose, hat, heels, and gloves), I took a subway from 181st Street to 59th Street, a second one to Times Square, a shuttle to Grand Central Station, and another subway down to the 20's.

I carried my lunch in a brown bag and ate it in the women's lounge, a tacky annex to the bathroom, with the sound of toilets flushing and paper towels being ripped from tin containers.

Weekends our Washington Heights apartment was invaded by our boyfriends, who all chipped in fifty cents apiece for Sunday dinner.

Lester came from Missouri to visit, and we went to Nick's or Eddie Condon's, in Greenwich Village, to hear jazz.

Dr. Waraich flew in, and we went to Hapsburg House, where the theme from *The Third Man* was played on the zither, or to Lüchow's, where a violinist played at your table while you ate sauerbraten with potato dumplings.

I couldn't get an agent, so I began sending out manuscripts under my roommates' names. I wanted a variety of names, and I wanted to be sure the manuscripts were safely returned to our mailbox.

I wrote anything and everything in an effort to get published. I wrote confession stories, articles, "slick" stories for the women's magazines, poetry and fillers.

One manuscript was returned from *Your Life* magazine with a hopeful letter, telling me that with a little revision, they might publish it. It was one of the ones sent out under a roommate's name.

She hit the roof when she saw the title: "Masturbation Is Normal."

After that, none of my roommates wanted their names on my work.

I did a revision, used my own name with a slight misspelling, and got the piece back with a "Sorry!" across the rejection slip.

———————

I was beginning to lose hope; I also lost my job.

In a year's time, I went from Dutton to Compton Advertising Company, to a medical house publishing *The Review of Gastroenterology* and *The Proctology Review*, to Fawcett Publications, fired almost as soon as I was hired.

Meanwhile, I'd found a way to get an agent: I'd become my own agent, print up stationery with my name on it and "Literary Agent," and send out stories under pseudonyms.

My pseudonyms were my clients.

On lunch breaks from Fawcett Publications, I visited editors and talked about Laura Winston (who wrote slicks for women's magazines), Mamie Stone (who wrote confessions), Edgar Stone, her "husband" (who wrote detective stories), and Winslow Albert (who wrote articles). . . . They were all me.

Finally, Fawcett fired me, tired of my two- and three-hour lunch breaks.

I sold three hundred shares of stock in Lockheed that my father'd given me for graduation, and made a bargain with my roommates.

I'd work full time as a free-lance writer/agent, paying rent, if they'd pay for the food I'd cook for them every night.

When I ran out of money, I'd go back to work.

It was 1951.

Weekdays I'd work on my writing, quitting in time to fix things like tuna casserole (mushroom soup, a can of peas, a can of tuna, and macaroni) for my roommates when they came home from their offices.

Weekends I'd go on dates to hear Charlie Parker play at Birdland, or to eat enchiladas at Mexican Gardens in the Village, or to Joe King's Rathskeller to sing and drink beer, and in nice weather we'd sit at The Brevoort's sidewalk cafe on lower Fifth Avenue.

On April 20, 1951, a letter came in the mail from the *Ladies' Home Journal*, to Marijane Meaker, Literary Agent, saying they were going to buy Laura Winston's story.

I raced to the phone to call my roommates.

I was so excited that I believed they were paying seventy-five dollars for the story.

No one, in any office in New York City, was at their desks. General Douglas MacArthur was being welcomed in New York City with an enormous ticker-tape parade!

When my roommates finally came home and read the acceptance letter themselves, one said, "It isn't seventy-five dollars they're paying you. It's seven hundred and fifty dollars!"

That night I took everyone out to dinner to Ruby Foo's for egg rolls, duckling chop suey, beef with snow-pea pods, et cetera, et cetera.

I'd earned enough to keep on writing for another six months.

I was on my way!

In September 1951, when my story was published, I opened to the table of contents and cried out, "Look, there's my name with John P. Marquand's and Dorothy Thompson's!"

"There's Laura Winston's name," a roommate said, "and there's your picture, with Laura Winston's name under it!"

On pages 46 and 47, there was a large illustration depicting three characters from my story.

The *Journal* Presents

LAURA WINSTON

And

Her First Published Story

'DEVOTEDLY, PATRICK HENRY CASEBOLT

It began:

A Paul Jones is a deviation of the old game of musical chairs, only instead of sitting on what you are in front of when the music stops, you dance with it. That was how I first met Patrick Henry Casebolt. It happened that warm September afternoon Wood Hollow Hall gave its initial tea dance of the year—a fearfully boring affair in the arid surroundings of the gymnasium.

Promptly at one-forty-five, the cadets from nearby Hillside Academy had massed in platoons and marched down the hill to be our guests—white-gloved, red-faced and grumbling.

The pod of M. E. Kerr was there already, in 1951, although it . was twenty-one years before it would shake itself loose from its shell and emerge full-blown.

Before Kerr, most of my work was written under the pseudonym Vin Packer, and many were paperback originals. Packer became a writer of suspense eventually, solely because I'd heard that *The New York Times'* mystery columnist, Anthony Boucher, would review paperbacks. Encouraged by his reviews of my work, I stayed in the field about ten years before going on to hardcover under my own name, Meaker.

Kerr came along later, and I feel a great deal of satisfaction being her.

Kids write and tell you what they think.

"When I see your name on the cover of books," a kid wrote me once, "I know that half the time they're good."

Another kid wrote saying, "Dear M. E. Kerr, we were forced to read you in English class."

What more could a writer ask for than a captive audience?

THE END